Setting the Record Straight

An Introduction to the History and Evolution
of Women's Professional Achievement

Setting the Record Straight

An Introduction to the History and Evolution of Women's Professional Achievement

Betty Reynolds, Ph.D.
Jill Tietjen, P.E.

white apple press
Denver

white apple press
1836 Blake St.
Denver, CO 80202
mailroom@penclay.com

Copyright 2001 by Betty Reynolds and Jill Tietjen. All rights reserved, including the right of reproduction in whole or in part in any form.

white apple press books are available at special discounts for reprint editions, bulk purchases, sales promotions, fund raising and educational purchases. Contact: Sales Department, white apple press, Finance Station, P.O. Box 480151, Denver, CO 80202; salesdepartment@penclay.com

Library of Congress Cataloging-in-Publication Data

Reynolds, Betty, 1925-
    Setting the record straight : an introduction to the history and evolution of women's professional achievement / Betty Reynolds, Jill Tietjen.
    p. cm.
Includes bibliographical references and index.
ISBN 0-9644849-5-1 (alk. paper)
    1. Women--United States--History. 2. Women--United States--Social conditions--History. 3. Women's rights--United States--History. I. Tietjen, Jill, 1954- II. Title.

HQ1150 .R495 2001
305.4'0973--dc21
                                      2001016240

Printed in the United States of America
Cover design by Ellen Reindeau

The paper in this book meets the guidelines for permanence and durability of the Committee on Production Guidelines for Book Longevity of the Council on Library Resources.

∞

Printed on Recycled Paper

To Cassie and Ashlie

—Betty Reynolds, Ph.D.

With deepest gratitude to Alexis Swoboda, my dear friend and Society of Women Engineers' colleague, who planted the seed

—Jill S. Titjen, P.E.

Contents

Preface ix

Acknowledgements xi

Introduction 1

Chapter One: Setting the Stage 9

Chapter Two: Preparing to Fight 37

Chapter Three: Women Attempt to Reform Soceity 67

Chapter Four: Gaining a Foothold 105

Chapter Five: Making Progress 129

Chapter Six: Battling Still 151

Notes 167

Bibliography 203

Index 217

Preface

Why worry about women's equality now, when women seem to have it made? They're represented in just about every profession; they hold positions of political power; it's a given for most people that women and girls are as capable and smart as men and boys. Though these statements may be true, women's equality is not as uncontroversial as it may at first appear. It's one thing for women to be represented at the lower echelons of the work place and the government. But if we examine who's in charge, it's still men. In the United States (and most other countries), men overwhelmingly hold the positions of power as heads of state. Think of the president and vice president of the United States. Not only has the president never been a woman, but neither the president nor the vice president has ever been a man of color, or a man who is Jewish or Buddhist, for instance. Clearly, prejudice has not died, even as it has receded in comparison to past years.

This book, and those in the series that follow, explores the reasons why women are where they are today in the United States. While our focus is primarily on professional working women, in this introductory book in particular, we will take a look at the history (or herstory, some might say) that has brought us to contemporary times. How did women go from being forbidden from owning anything at all to one-third of self-employed business owners being women?[1] How did women go from not being able to vote or even address Congress, to holding 72 congressional seats in 2001.

Times have changed essentially because laws changed. And laws were changed because some people cared enough to work very hard to change peoples' minds. The pages that follow tell some of the many stories in this most important struggle. Indeed, as we embark upon a promising new century, it's time to set the record straight.

Acknowledgements

As with any undertaking of this sort, many people provided support, assistance, and encouragement. We thank the following and apologize in advance for any errors or omissions.

From the Denver Public Library, Elena Wenzel. From the U.S. Department of Labor, Michael Williams. Eleanor Babco, from the CPST.

The accountants: Lynda Munion Dennis, CPA, Nancy Heimer, CPA, Cheryl Lehman, CPA, David Rediger, CPA.

The lawyers: Linda Bernard, J.D., LLM, Leslie Blau, Esq., Sally Lee Foley, Esq., Connie H. King, Esq., Dean Gail E. Sasnett, Janice L. Sperow, Esq., Heather Vargas, Esq.

The engineers: Dr. Mary Anderson-Rowland, Sherita Ceasar, Patricia L. Eng, P.E., Carrie Kessler, Rona Prufer, Sandra Scanlon, P.E., Dr. Margaret Wheatley.

From Women in Engineering Programs: Dr. Suzanne Brainard, Dr. Jane Daniels, Dr. Suzanne Laurich-McIntyre.

And other friends and supporters: Daylemarie Axtell, William Brentholz, Mary S. Dolan, Grace Fields, Dr. Frank Franco, Peggy L. Golden, Dr. Vance W. Grant, Kathy Grimm, Katherine Hager, Barbara Hirst, Phyllis Kopriva, Debby Lithgow, Ellen T. Mayer, Sue McGinley,

Albreta Merrit, Ramona Perry-Jones, Robert Polk, Sharon Madison Polk, Barbara Smith, Pat Snyder, and Professor Paula D. Thomas.

We'd also like to thank our publisher, Kendall Bohannon, and our editor, Wendy DuBow, at White Apple Press for believing in and supporting this series.

Betty Reynolds, Ph.D., Jill S. Tietjen, P.E.

Introduction

We are in the midst of a sweeping shift in human potential. The movement of women from a second-class, subjugated social status to a more equal and respected existence will have a far-reaching impact on human society. While this shift is by no means complete nor ubiquitous, the progress made in the latter half of the twentieth century is mind-boggling compared with women's progress up to that point.

If you were a female born in 1799 in the newly established United States of America, you could expect to marry young, have children early, work hard around the house, and then die.[1] On the other hand, if you were a male born in 1799 in these same United States, you could expect to marry young, have children early, work hard *outside* the house, and then die.

If you were a girl born in 1899 in the increasingly conservative United States, you could expect to marry young, have children early, work hard around the house, and then die. And if you were a boy born at the same time in the same place, you could expect to marry young, have children early, work hard *outside* the house, and then die.

If you were female in either century, you could not expect to willingly postpone having children, nor limit the number of children you did have. Nor could you vote in the new republic. On the other hand, if you were a white male, you could expect to be educated (at least on par with our current grade school standards), to own your house and property, to vote, and to have very little to do with raising your children.

If you were a girl born in 1999 in the U.S., you could expect to marry when you wished (or not), have children (or not), work hard around the house (or not), work hard outside the house (or not), and then die. You could also expect to acquire the education you desire (presuming you have the financial means), to own your house and property (again presuming you have the financial means), and to vote.

If you were a boy born in 1999, you could do all of the above as well. So, have we arrived at an egalitarian equilibrium among the sexes? Some would say yes. Those who continue to experience or study discrimination would argue that we have not.

Let's examine a typical (albeit fictional) situation: a corporate boardroom meeting in the U.S. at the beginning of the new millennium. Perhaps from this, we can assess with a fair amount of accuracy just how far our society has come.[2]

The male chairman of the Board of Directors calls the meeting of the Board to order. The two women and 12 men at the table turn their attention to the agenda. During the course of their meeting, they will discuss weighty issues, including a potential acquisition by the corporation; corporate officers will be making some presentations to the Board as it covers the various issues. Those officers include five men and one woman. Out of a total of 20 officers in the corporation, three are women.

The nominating committee presentation on suitable candidates to fill the vacancy on the Board includes five candidates—all men. The discussion about who would take over if the CEO were to leave focuses on two men.

The assistant corporate secretary and two administrative assistants are in the room at all times to handle presentation materials, take minutes, handle travel concerns, relay messages, and attend to food and beverages. These individuals are all female.

One item on the agenda is an announcement that the company was named one of the best employers for working mothers by a national magazine. The company has a documented sexual harassment policy that it enforces, offers an on-site day care center, has a liberal maternity leave policy, encourages employees to use flexible work arrangements, provides workplace lactation centers, and 35 percent of its managers are female.

The female officers and the women on the Board know, however, that they represent a small percentage of the total number of women who work for the company. Although at some levels of the organization, gender equality appears to have been achieved, they know that few women hold high level positions. They've heard the all-too familiar refrain, "We just can't find any qualified women." They also know that there are many qualified women; some don't have the same types of credentials or approaches as their male counterparts; some are too pretty; some are not pretty enough. Factors like these shouldn't matter to a hiring supervisor, but they still influence decisions. Other women never even have a chance to be discriminated against at this level because they are too busy working a dead-end job in order to support their children.

Notwithstanding the current inequities, women have indeed come a long way, and America is a much more egalitarian society than it was in its infancy. But we still have a long way to go until perceptions of race and gender do not pre-determine what you can achieve in our society.

New Beginnings, Old Ways

Women who first came to the new country possessed many of the same expectations as the men they accompanied from the old country. Both wanted a better life with more freedom of thought and action. However, in the new world, women were denied the rights that men—i.e., Caucasian men who owned property—took for granted. Women were not allowed to be educated; they had no political voice; and they were barred from participation in the public sphere. Women were allowed to control neither the wages they earned nor property they owned. They were unable to secure custody of their children in a divorce and were denied the right to vote. Early in colonial times, some talented and/or outspoken women were even persecuted as "witches."

It's clear from accounts of this period that the ideology of male superiority remained virtually unchallenged. The few women who dared to speak their minds about the treatment of women did not succeed in altering traditional attitudes toward "a woman's place." Public opinion was not in their favor, and traditional attitudes supporting "the cult of true womanhood" lingered for centuries.[3]

Men were dominant—they ruled the home, church and state, and the workplace was their public domain. Women were presumed to be inferior and subordinate. The female sphere was narrowly defined as domestic, and the female role specifically ordained as wife and mother. The feminine values of piety, purity, obedience, and submissiveness were constantly reinforced in the home, in the church, and in the popular writings of the day. Women were warned to avoid certain books that might fill their heads with radical ideas, to bear problems with their husbands quietly, and not to expect much in the way of conjugal and domestic happiness.

The workplace was the exclusive domain of men during most periods of American history. The societal norms that dictated a woman's proper place were applied, except in the case of war and worker shortages.

Benjamin Franklin wrote in his *Reflections on Courtship and Marriage* in 1746 that female education should focus on preparation for marriage and motherhood, as well as household management. Franklin's wife, Deborah, not only managed the household during his periodic absences, but also managed the printing business. Although some women seemed to rebel at being limited to the "domestic" pursuits, there appears to be little evidence that before the 1780s American women perceived their lack of education as a situation that required a remedy.[4]

The only professions that were deemed acceptable for women were teaching and midwifery. And, as we shall see in the pages that follow, even these professions began to exclude women as time passed. Educational deficiencies seriously hampered women interested in any of the "learned" professions. Women were not permitted to attend the few, all-male institutions of higher education that existed before the Civil War. Even female teachers had little formal training beyond an elementary level of education.

Governmental, corporate, and political decision-makers in the U.S. have tended to be individuals from these "learned" professions, such as lawyers, accountants, and engineers. Women were thus excluded from corporate, community, state, and national decision-making because of their exclusion from these fields and from voting. The professions also provided some of the best paying occupations. Exclusion of women from the professions precluded their ability to achieve financial independence as well, so a husband was necessary for financial support.

Women played some active roles in other areas of business and commerce throughout the seventeenth and eighteenth centuries: Women worked together with men to ensure the success of mutual business enterprises, and often functioned as shopkeepers and innkeepers. They also engaged in a number of trades as tanners, brewers, lumberjacks, printers, woodworkers, and so on. These women were apparently successful in defying tradition without the customary restrictions. Generally, though, it is because they worked side-by-side with a male family member or spouse, or were widows running the family business.[5]

As women began to lobby for the right to vote, and the right to be educated, they encountered much resistance. The time was ripe for the entrance of the early feminists who fought for rights on all fronts. Early feminists came from a variety of different backgrounds, and included African-American as well as Caucasian women, and some of the few women who had managed to infiltrate the professions. Not surprisingly, these women did not always agree on the most important cause to espouse at any given time.

Nonetheless, their contributions to the reform movements, individually and collectively, helped to create many of the defining moments in American history. Women were ardent supporters and activists in the fight to free slaves, and almost single-handedly fought for women's right to vote.

It is not always clear who among these early pioneers was first to have achieved a particular goal or honor, but the distinction of being "first" is not what is important. What really matters is how much they accomplished despite limited resources, lack of modern-day communication channels, intimidation by men, and lack of support by other women. Their often unappreciated efforts pioneered the way for generations of women to follow, and this is the inspiration that makes their stories worth telling.

History Lends Context

As we enter the twenty-first century, women outnumber men in entering and completing college. Women comprise almost half of entering law students and over 40 percent of those pursuing medical degrees.[6] In spite of these accomplishments in the educational sphere, no woman has been president of the United States; women constitute a significantly smaller percentage of Congress than their numbers might lead one to expect; and most of the corporate and community decision-makers are men. Why haven't education and entry into the professions led to more equality? To answer this question, we must look to the nature of the transformation that we have undergone thus far.

America's consumer-oriented culture has picked up on the economic potential of the emerging zeitgeist. Catchy slogans, bumper stickers and sound bites declared women's new-found sense of empowerment. Phrases like "You go, girl!" and "Girls Rule!" have found their way onto t-shirts, bumper stickers and TV commercials.

Indeed, popular culture tends to support the idea that the shift to an enlightened collective understanding of gender equality has already been accomplished, and that there are no longer any obstacles to women's advancement. Women's rights have been accomplished, so the underlying issues can be relegated to history books, with all the other cultural baggage, such as racism, that has been "overcome" and is now a part of our past, not our present.

And, to be fair, the dynamics of political power have begun to change, as politicians court the increasingly vocal, powerful—and organized—women voters. Social and economic philosophies have begun to espouse the idea of maximizing human and economic potential through incorporating egalitarian gender principles into virtually every aspect of American life.

Despite the prevailing sentiments, however, high-profile incidents in the last decade of the twentieth century indicated that the enlightened collective psyche that we had already begun to take for granted is, in reality, not fully developed. From the Clarence Thomas Supreme Court confirmation hearings to deep-seated sexism in the military and double standards in the media, it's clear that we're not as far along as our rhetoric suggests.

This disparity suggests that the development of egalitarian gender attitudes is only superficial, more a product of political and economic opportunism than enlightened and significant social change. The reason for this is that fundamental learning never took place. The pseudo-education stimulated by pop culture was ill-equipped to do the job that it suggested we had already done. Consequently, much of our society has little sense of the struggle involved in getting where we are today and no sense of the evolution of an egalitarian ideal. We lack history and context.

This book is the first in a series that explores the history of women in the "learned professions." This introductory volume provides an overview of the development of women's rights in the US from the colonial period to the beginning of the twenty-first century. With a more studied perspective of the people and events that have contributed to the current state of women's rights and professional status, we can gain a more thorough understanding of the significance of the achievements thus far, and consequently, be better equipped to tackle the challenges we still face. Subsequent books in this series highlight the struggles and successes of women as they entered the fields of engineering, accounting, law, medicine, science, and academia, with high hopes for accomplishment, recognition, and the ability to contribute to the advancement of humanity.

Chapter One
Setting the Stage

> *It is possible, reading standard histories, to forget half the population of the country. The explorers were men, the landholders and merchants men, the political leaders men, the military figures men. The very invisibility of women, the overlooking of women, is a sign of their submerged status.*[1]

Colonization

The women and men who first colonized America left Europe in the early 1600s to find a better life in the new country. They arrived seeking religious freedom, opportunities that were no longer limited by class distinctions (as had been the case in the old country), and maybe even gold.[2]

Although it is as difficult to generalize about the position of women in colonial society as it is to generalize about the position of American women today, a reasonable assumption is that distinct differences in roles could be found between economically distinct segments of society. It was one thing to be the mistress of a large plantation, or the wife of a wealthy Eastern merchant. It was quite another to be a pioneer woman on the frontier, or a slave or servant girl.[3] Though there was an unmistakable difference between the ease with which each of these groups of women lived their lives, they all had one thing in common: Regardless of social station, all women were legally "chattel," and thus subordinate to men.

Religious beliefs and a general lack of education among the populace further conspired to "keep women in their place."

The laws and customs that took hold first in the original 13 colonies were based on English Common Law. According to English Common Law, women's social status was acquired either by birth or marriage. Women had many duties befitting their station, but few, if any rights; they were trapped in a condition known now as "civil death."[4] Married women were particularly affected by this condition. They were not allowed to be in control of their own property or wages, and had no legal rights separate from their husbands.

"Civil death" applied to women in all political matters, including the right to vote. A few scattered instances of women being allowed to vote have been recorded as some enlightened communities enfranchised all property owners of either sex. However the limited voting privilege enjoyed by a few white women only lasted for a short period, as state after state rescinded the vote for women, ending with New Jersey, in 1807.[5] Suffrage for women was not broached as a universal right until many decades later.[6]

Along with law, religion was a potent force in maintaining women's subordinate position in colonial society. The different religious factions may have disagreed on their religious beliefs and practices, but they never faltered on the one belief they held in common: it was God's will that women should occupy a role secondary to that of men. The perceived limitations of a woman's mind and body ordained her submissive, subservient role to her father, her brother and her husband.[7]

Minority men and women had even less social status than white women. In fact, their status was such that little is known about most minorities in colonial times, and unless mentioned otherwise, the history that is provided in this volume reflects history as written by and about Caucasian Americans.[8]

The risk was high for those women who dared to challenge religion or the perceived superiority of men, as one "rebel," Anne Hutchinson, learned when she openly challenged authorities of the Massachusetts colony. Mistress Anne was a religious woman, mother of 13 children and a knowledgeable healer. She had a loyal band of followers, primarily women (but some men), who listened when she insisted that ordinary people had the right to interpret the Bible for themselves and that women should have a voice in church affairs. Mistress Anne was vocal about these beliefs from 1634 when she arrived in Boston through both a civil trial (charge: rebellion against authority) and religious proceedings (charge: heresy) from 1637 to 1638. In 1637, she was found guilty on all charges and sentenced to banishment from the colony. In 1638, she was expelled from the church.[9]

Another outspoken woman, Mary Dyer, who had challenged the court during Anne Hutchinson's trial, was later charged with heresy and hanged along with two other women for their crimes of "rebellion, sedition, and presumptuously obtruding themselves."[10] Men might be charged with rebellion or sedition, but certainly they would never have been charged with "presumptuously obtruding" themselves! The men in authority were able to keep women in their "place" through chains of law and religion.

During colonial times, education beyond the elementary level was denied to females. Jean-Jacques Rousseau (1712-1778) captures the general philosophy of the time: "The whole education of women ought to be relative to men. To please them, to be useful to them, to make themselves loved and honored by them."[11]

There was more involved in denying education to females than simply sexist attitudes—although this was a factor. Formal schooling was rare during colonial days, and whatever education was available was not free. Public schools as we know them today did not exist. Most families could not afford the cost of the few high-priced private schools available to girls—even if they were in favor of having their girls educated. The only option available was "home teaching" to instill a few basic skills thought to be necessary. Learning the domestic arts—cooking, sewing, home care, child care—was essential. Acquiring reading skills helped young females to fulfill their Christian obligation to read the Bible. Pseudo-scientific arguments popular at the time proposed that higher education was detrimental to women, i.e., women had to devote so much of their bodily energy to their reproductive function that they were unable to develop their intellectual abilities. If women insisted upon straining their brains, they could become sterile or give birth to unhealthy children.[12]

Females were not the only group denied access to education. To be formally educated—especially beyond the high school level—was a rare privilege throughout most of Western history and exclusively granted to affluent males. The few private colleges established during this period, such as Harvard, Yale, Princeton, and Dartmouth, excluded women.[13] The literacy rate for white women reached about 40 percent, as compared with about 80 percent of the white male population by the end of the colonial period.[14] Following a long-established tradition brought over from Europe, free public education was not made available to the American public for many years to come. At the time the Constitution was adopted, few colonials had attended any kind of school.[15]

Education for African-American women was in an even worse state as many colonists believed that women of color could not be educated. Phillis Wheatley (c. 1753-1784), an early example of an African-American woman who was obviously quite capable of creative work, was captured by slave traders and sold in the Boston slave market at the age of seven. Wheatley's owners—themselves both educated and kind—treated her as one of the family and gave her the best possible schooling. She was encouraged to use her gifts as a Latin scholar and poet, and won interest and recognition both at home and abroad. When an ode she wrote and dedicated to George Washington ("To His Excellency General Washington") was published in *Pennsylvania Magazine*, he invited her to visit his headquarters in Cambridge—and she did. Despite her fame, there was no real place in the colonial world for a woman of color like Phillis Wheatley. She died destitute in 1784, her husband had deserted her, her three children had died, and she was buried in a pauper's grave, although her fame as a poet has survived to the present.[16]

American Revolution

Although the Declaration of Independence (1776) and the U.S. Constitution (1787) contain language that seems to imply equality for all people, these documents and the laws they generated were deemed not to apply to various categories of humanity. In fact, the founding fathers failed to include at least five groups in either the Declaration or the Constitution. Slaves, indentured servants, Native Americans, white men without property, and women were left out of the documents that established the basis for free Americans. The exclusion of these groups from the political process effectively eliminated a large segment of the country's population from a share in the newly won freedom.[17]

The signing of the Declaration of Independence in 1776 did not change the status quo, nor was that the intention of the signers. Thomas Jefferson's memorable expression, "All men are created equal," was not meant to be taken literally (except in the sense of applying strictly to men). Jefferson himself said that "women would be too wise to wrinkle their foreheads with politics."[18]

Abigail Adams wrote a letter to her husband, John, a delegate to the Continental Congress and later the second U.S. president, in 1776, pleading with him to offer women the voice of representation in the new code of laws about to be drafted.[19] Her husband shrugged off her suggestion and replied, "Depend on it, we know better than to repeal our masculine systems."[20]

Women did not lose their legal status when the Constitution was ratified in 1787 because they had never had any. In a sense, though, they were left in a worse position than some of the other excluded groups. White men without property could eventually acquire property and then join the privileged male class. Indentured male servants could work off their indenture, acquire property and thereafter be entitled to these rights. Slaves were eventually freed, although male and female former slaves had many issues to overcome. Women, of any ethnicity, had few options to change their legal status. They were left out of the political process altogether and lacked the public support necessary to change the system.

In the face of the many powerful messages constantly reinforcing the inequality of the sexes during the eighteenth century, it was unlikely that any change in women's position would take place. Change, however, was inevitable. Ideas of female equality were in the air even before the Revolution, and many of these ideas began to surface in periodicals published during that period. Thomas Paine, for example, became an outspoken critic of the subjugation of women, and an article written in his *Pennsylvania Magazine* before the Revolution condemned the "civil death" of women. The article stated, in part, that women were robbed of their freedom and will by the laws and were surrounded by judges who were "at once tyrants and their seducers."[21]

Some women may have agreed with these radical ideas, but they were reluctant to express their rebelliousness openly. Dissatisfaction was generally expressed by a few privileged women in their "day journals," or in letters written to other women of their social class with similar inclinations. Feminists' views were outside the realm of both political and social discourse, and concerns about the social and political position of women would not become well-defined issues until the mid-nineteenth century.[22]

However inadvertently, the door to political discourse had been left open by the authors of the Constitution, as they consistently used the gender-neutral word "person" rather than "man" in its then common generic sense.[23] This language aided in gaining slaves and, eventually, women their Constitutional rights.

Did women have inalienable rights? Mary Wollstonecraft thought so, and she used her powerful writing to stimulate thought on a new order. Her pioneering book, *A Vindication of the Rights of Women*, published in England in 1792, is the document from which the women's rights movement is said to be dated.[24] The book is thought to have been written as a response to the English conservative Edmund Burke, who wrote "a woman is but an animal, and an animal not of the highest order."

Wollstonecraft did not dignify this insult with a direct rejoinder, but instead addressed her remarks directly to women. She warned women that the refinements and sentiments that characterized women were a sign of weakness that made them objects of contempt by men. She suggested that women consider a better ambition: obtaining character as a human being.[25]

At about the same time as Wollstonecraft was writing, Judith Sargent Murray began to emphasize the benefit of education to women. In 1790, she published the first feminist tract to appear in print in the U.S., *On The Equality of the Sexes*. In her book, she protested the lack of equality in education between boys and girls. Six years later, she was still going strong and wrote another treatise. Murray wrote extolling the importance of education in preparing women for independent thought, broader rights and opportunities.[26]

Although ideas about female education reform had begun to take root before the Revolution, they did not bear fruit until after the war was over. The founding fathers of the New Republic began to search for ways to improve education for young females. The first reformers were influential males who questioned the traditional approach to education. There were, however, wide differences in their views concerning its potential value—ranging from ultra-conservative to more moderate. Noah Webster, author of the first American dictionary, for example, stressed the "domestic value" of educating women. Others, such as Benjamin Rush, a physician and scientist involved in women's education, emphasized the importance of education in preparing women to raise sons as loyal and responsible citizens. The opinions of Webster and Rush reflected a resurgence of the fundamental traditionalism that had dominated the earlier colonial period.[27] Nevertheless, that prominent men would concern themselves with such an allegedly trivial matter as female education lent credibility to the movement. Their prestige helped to give it standing, but it took a group of enlightened and dedicated women to bring the ideas of improved education to reality. The idea that female education was a patriotic duty became more firmly entrenched between

1776 and 1840.[28] During this period, a marked improvement was seen in the kind and amount of schooling that girls were to receive.

Female Seminaries

Female private schools and female seminaries, also known as "dame schools," came into being some time around the 1780s and grew in number during the early part of the nineteenth century.[29] Although attendance was limited to the well-to-do while poorer women still received a limited education or none at all, these schools contributed to women's educational history in that they were organized schools for the purpose of educating females. And the schools filled another need: occupational choice was limited for women, so being the "mistress" of a dame school was an excellent source of income for spinsters and widows with children to raise.

Most of the dame schools did provide a rudimentary education for the development of genteel young ladies. The training mainly consisted of a few domestic subjects such as embroidery, painting, singing and playing the harpsichord[30], but the major emphasis was on the development of social graces to enhance "feminine charms." The purpose of this social training was to ensure that graduates would attract a "proper suitor" to marry.

A few of the more adventuresome "dames" expanded the basic curriculum to include a smattering of language, history, and an exposure to elementary science. These head mistresses were careful to disguise their tentative academic offerings in their advertisements for fear of offending potential patrons. The wealthy often paid large sums for the privilege of having their daughters attend a school with a reputation for "respectability." Exposing young ladies to "advanced" learning was not respectable. The notion of producing "learned" young ladies, was unacceptable, especially as it might whet their appetites for more education. The dames who followed the traditional model provided a semblance of education for females but did little to further the development of quality education for women in America.[31]

By 1812, education for women had received widespread attention throughout the country, but there had been little progress.[32] Sarah Pierce, principal of the Academy at Litchfield, told her female students in 1818 that the equality of intellect of men and women implied equality of educational goals and opportunities.[33] Equality of male and female intellect and education of women, however, were still viewed as radical ideas in the early 1800s.

The First Coeducational College

Early education pioneers were successful in gaining women access to secondary education, including the opening of public schools for girls. Massachusetts took the lead and opened the first in Worcester in 1824. New York City and Boston followed with a comparable school system in 1826.[34] By 1850, most sizeable cities could boast at least one girls' public school, even though there continued to be a disproportionately higher number of schools for boys. Not a single college, however, admitted women until 1837, when Oberlin began to accept anyone who sought higher education—regardless of race, color, or sex.[35]

Oberlin was founded in 1833 as a seminary for men, but later developed into a full-fledged college. James Fairchild, chief spokesperson for the school, was able to argue convincingly to the trustees that society had the moral obligation to educate women. Convinced by Fairchild's argument, the trustees agreed to liberalize the school's admission policy.[36]

Some would argue that Oberlin's motivation was questionable. Oberlin's mission, from the beginning, was to train evangelical ministers, and having female students on campus would contribute to the success of this mission.[37] It was believed that women were likely to exert a "civilizing influence" on neophyte ministers. Through their contacts with the female students, the young ministers might learn the social graces necessary to appeal to congregations made up largely of women. Whatever the motive, an opportunity had been made available to women that had not existed before.

At first, Oberlin's open-door policy lacked the essential elements to be considered "equal opportunity." Women were only allowed to take a condensed "literary arts" courses in deference to their "smaller brain." It was presumed that this physiological difference would not permit women to tackle the more complex subjects offered to the men. Fortunately, these sex-dictated curriculum limitations lasted only a short time, and a woman was permitted to graduate with a regular bachelor's degree in 1841. She was followed by Antoinette Brown, who later was to become the first woman ordained as a minister, and the influential women's rights activist Lucy Stone. Despite the fame that came later for these two graduates, they were not recognized as "model students" during their stay at Oberlin. Their scholastic achievements were noteworthy, but both of them were always in trouble with the authorities because of their feminist views and outspoken ways.[38]

The American education reform movement caught the attention of critics and visitors from Europe. These foreign reformers (who had plenty to scrutinize in their own countries) found much to condemn about the quality of U.S. education. One of these critics, George Combe, a Scottish phrenologist, traveled throughout the United States from 1838 to 1840 to inspect the school system. One of the instances of sex discrimination he pointed out was the differential pay between female and male teachers. He found that male teachers in Massachusetts averaged a little over $185 a year, above board, while female teachers earned only about $65 a year above board. Combe was appalled by both wages, saying that the sums were inexcusably low in a country where the average laborer earned $1 per day.[39]

In Combe's report on the Massachusetts school system, he expressed disappointment that the state made no provision for the education of girls beyond high school. There were about eight seminaries and colleges for men—many of them well endowed, and all receiving state aid. He was unable to find a single seminary that had either been endowed or permanently established for the education of young women. As he continued his travels, he found an even worse situation in school systems across the country.40

Minority Education

Not surprisingly, the path to education was much more perilous for minorities than for other segments of the population in early America.41 Gender, social class, religion, geographic regions, and race were the dominant factors that influenced access to education. These factors—operating singly or in tandem—determined the educational fate of minority women. Beliefs about women of color's alleged intellectual inferiority probably had the most impact. The logic is inescapable when viewed from the perspective of the prevailing racist and sexist mindset of that day. A white woman was perceived as being mentally incapable of absorbing the same education as a man, and non-whites were considered inferior to whites. Thus, minority females had the least possible potential for mental growth. As a consequence, notions about educating African-American females generally were not entertained.

There were, however, exceptions to this rule. The dominant white society's self-interest dictated that some attention should be given to the education of Native Americans and of African Americans, slave or free. Primarily, the purpose behind the few limited opportunities made available was to impose social control rather than to enhance social progress.

Minorities themselves perceived education as the gateway to acceptance and potential advancement into mainstream society. Slaves, in particular, considered school the first step away from bondage. Fortunately, there were individuals and groups among the colonists and New Republicans who agreed with them and felt it was their Christian obligation to provide the opportunity. Both Native Americans and African-Americans benefited from the teachings of missionaries and sought other avenues as well to help educate their own people.

Missionaries were already engaged in literacy and religious training among Native Americans when the Continental Congress decided that support from Native Americans would be advantageous in the revolt against the British. Ministers and teachers were sent as a gesture of goodwill to gain Indian support. After the Revolution, the Indian education policy was continued to maintain goodwill of potential allies as well as ensure the signing of treaties, and to open up more lands to white settlers. It was thought that educating the Native Americans would turn them from nomads into civilized farmers. The Cherokees took full advantage of having access to education. One Cherokee, Sequoyah, designed a phonetic alphabet representing the Cherokee language. By 1828, the Cherokees had their own printing press and were publishing a newspaper, religious tracts, and a Bible, and thousands could read and write.[42]

Education for the African-American population during the colonial and New Republic period was a more controversial issue than was education for women. White women had one strike against them—their gender. On the other hand, African Americans had three factors to contend with: their status as "slave" or "free," their geographical location, and the self-interests of the different factions involved. Some slave owners educated their slaves with certain essential skills to promote economic efficiency. However "slave codes" prohibited the education of slaves, so those who violated the code were subject to legal penalties and social ostracism.[43]

Plantation owners were aware that slaves were quite capable of learning. The African-American leaders of the abolitionist movement were literate, skilled tradesmen, and artisans. In addition, the Quakers were particularly persistent in educating African Americans, as they believed that education was integral to abolition. During the early decades of the nineteenth century, the Quakers established adult education programs in Philadelphia and New York.[44] Free African Americans established "Mutual Improvement Societies"—mostly in secret—that focused on race uplifting, with education being a primary goal. Societies were formed in Rhode Island in 1780; in New Orleans in 1783; in Philadelphia in 1787; and in Boston in 1796. The first African-American National Convention was held in 1794 with many white supporters in attendance. The delegates adopted a platform proposing that emancipation could only be achieved through education. However, even in the

North, where slavery was abolished state by state over a 50-year period beginning in 1790, African-American children were barred from public schools in most locations. Thus, by the time of emancipation in 1865, only about seven percent of adult African Americans were literate.[45]

Industrial Revolution and Westward Expansion

Westward expansion and the beginning of industrial production outside the home created a number of changes in the way Americans lived their lives and had a significant impact on women. As the economy and population expanded, so did the need for teachers and cheap labor to operate the factories. Men generally sought more lucrative occupations, or expected to be paid more than the wages paid to women. There was a plentiful supply of women with limited prospects of marriage, or other means of supporting themselves. Consequently, it became more socially and economically feasible for women to work outside the home.[46]

The first power-driven loom was set up in Massachusetts in 1817. As others were put into operation, it became obvious to the factory owners that women could use the same nimbleness and skills employed in spinning and weaving in the home in the textile industry factories.[47] At the same time that single women were in demand as textile factory workers, however, married women were still under pressure to stay in the home and tend to "wife and mother" duties.[48]

Because large numbers of women were employed by the new textile factories, industrialization played a crucial role in setting the stage for the first wave of the women's rights movement. Factory workers were forced to work under the most deplorable conditions imaginable, working 12 to 16 hours a day, earning as little as 25 cents a day—plus room and board. Some of these factory workers were even children, under the age of 18, and not protected by child labor laws since none yet existed. Some of the earliest industrial strikes took place in textile mills in the 1820s and 1840s to protest such conditions, and included male and female workers.[49]

As more women entered the work force, both as teachers and as factory workers, they became more economically independent. However, the lack of direct political influence constituted a powerful reason why women's wages had been kept at a minimum.[50] Many women began to believe that women having the vote would lead to a redress of many wrongs in American society and the economy. None yet were saying, however, that a woman was equal in every respect with a man.[51]

Catharine Beecher, an advocate of education for women and the sister of Harriet Beecher Stowe, strove to gain broad public sympathy by writing a number of articles criticizing the factory systems' treatment of women. A Female Labor Reform Association put out a series of tracts, speaking of the textile mill women as being nothing more nor less than slaves in every sense of the word, subject to the will and requirements of the "powers that be." Although sympathy was generated by these vivid accounts, the strikes were mostly unsuccessful, and working conditions for women and children did not immediately improve.[52]

Early feminists did not emerge from the women who worked in the factories during this period. When the textile mill women organized, they focused their grievances on being underpaid and overworked laborers—not on their status as women.[53] Industrialization was not very far along when the term "women's rights" was coined by Mary Wollstonecraft in 1792 in *The Vindication of the Rights of Women*.[54] Some historians have claimed that the new methods of production created during the Industrial Revolution reduced the amount of domestic work in the home, freeing women to engage in outside activities, such as reform movements. Other historians see this claim as exaggerated.

Men began to fear that they were losing their dominance; what with women entering the workplace, demanding to be paid fairly and not eagerly taking on all of the work around the house. As the role of women became increasingly ambiguous, pressures mounted to develop a set of ideas to keep women in their place. Consequently, the media began to stress the importance of women remaining home to care for children and to discharge their other domestic responsibilities.[55] The movement to bring back the old social controls prevailed over women's desire for freedom. The return of the cherished "Cult of Domesticity" helped to restore the stability that the dominant male society felt was essential for the burgeoning new nation. The fact remained that women working outside the home, and other forces that could not be easily contained, were moving women in other directions. Nevertheless, the image of the "stay-at-home" wife and mother continued to dog women's steps until well into the nineteenth century.[56]

Women's outcry for release from their bondage may have been only a soft whimper in 1820, but subversive seeds had been planted that would have far-reaching effects over the next 100 years. Women began to suspect that if they were so talented in home management, they could transfer these talents to other spheres.

Abolition

During the 60 years after the American Revolution, the stratification of people remained fairly static, not even approaching what we might think of as "equality" among different types of people. However, significant strides had been taken in the effort to abolish slavery—the abolitionist movement. And these efforts would also eventually lead to the women's rights movement.

In fact, some historians argue that the abolitionist movement was the most important factor to ignite the women's movement. Abolition, with its strong ethical and religious overtones, inevitably attracted women already enamored with the idea of the sanctity of the home. Women also were likely to react emotionally to the thought of slave mothers being separated from their children, and to the sexual exploitation of female slaves. Still another reason why slavery would push women toward feminism is that they became increasingly aware of the parallel between their own condition and that of slaves.[57]

Male abolitionists, on the other hand, were much more singleminded. They were deeply committed to the anti-slavery cause, but they were divided over the issue of whether females should be allowed to participate in the movement. One of the reasons for their hesitation is that they feared women's involvement would give the impression that the men advocated sexual equality, thus damaging their effectiveness. As a result, a fight between factions erupted to either accept or reject women on equal terms within the abolitionist movement—a disagreement that would resurface in the civil rights movement of the 1960s.

In the abolitionist movement, women demonstrated their dedication to the cause, working tirelessly alongside men to end the practice of slavery in America. Women's involvement in improving their own condition in life was in fact sparked by two very strong abolitionists—the Grimkë sisters, Sarah and Angelina. But most abolitionists failed to see the connection between rights for African-American men and women, and rights for all women. Equal rights did not have the meaningful resonance it does today.

Like the Grimkës, the women's rights pioneers who came after them, also worked hard volunteering for the antislavery movement. They bombarded Congress regularly with petitions to end slavery. At first the only goal of women—including such well-known feminists as Lucretia Mott, Elizabeth Cady Stanton, and Susan B. Anthony—was to end slavery. The connection between freeing slaves and ending their own bondage was to come later. Once the connection had been made, though, women began to work diligently on behalf of both causes until a major rift occurred between the abolitionist and suffragette ideologies.

The controversy, which had been brewing for some time, came to a head when the abolitionist society met in 1840. A floor fight among the delegates broke out over the right of women to take leadership positions in the organization. When a woman was appointed by the chairman to the business committee, the more conservative New York contingency seceded in protest. The dissenters formed a new organization, the American and Foreign Anti-Slavery Society, and specifically limited its membership to men. Although women were elected to the executive committee of what was left of the original organization, the affront of being denied equal participation left its mark. This occurrence, plus later events of a similar nature, ultimately led to the sprouting of the first organized women's rights efforts.[58]

During the same year of the abolitionist split, the original organization sent Lucretia Mott and Henry Stanton (on a honeymoon with his new bride, Elizabeth Cady) as their representatives to the World Anti-Slavery Convention in London. The convention refused to seat the female delegates; they were forced to sit in the gallery behind a screen, and not allowed to take any part in the proceedings. This intended slight by the all-male delegation was a fortuitous turn of events, for it was here that Lucretia Mott and Elizabeth Cady Stanton met for the first time. The two women, not allowed to take part in the proceedings, began to talk to each other. Mott was 20 years Cady Stanton's senior, and a persuasive speaker, who was able to convert the younger woman to the cause of women's rights. At the same time, the seed was planted to call the first women's rights convention at Seneca Falls.[59]

Declaration of Sentiments

"We hold these truths to be self-evident; that all men and women are created equal; that they are endowed by their Creator with certain inalienable rights; that among these are life, liberty and the pursuit of happiness; that to secure these rights governments are instituted, deriving their just powers from the consent of the governed."[60]

These words, obviously modified from the Declaration of Independence, are the opening words of the Declaration of Sentiments, the result of a Convention in Seneca Falls, New York held in 1848. The Convention, held twelve years before the Civil War, propelled the women's rights movement forward.

At the time of Seneca Falls, the nation was experiencing a tremendous acceleration of growth in size, population, and economic development. Women's rights were still ridiculed by the press, but accounts of settlers reaching California and the great Northwest became more newsworthy. By 1850, the growing work force in manufacturing of close to one million included over 200 thousand women—almost 24 percent of the total. Slavery was the great moral and economic issue of the day. It affected the wages of workers in the North as well as South. It also weighed heavily on the Southern white woman's ability to engage in the movement for greater equality that emerged among Northern women.

Northern women had more freedom to become involved in a broad range of intellectual and reform activities.

Ideas of equality date back to a much earlier period, but the Seneca Falls Convention, called by Elizabeth Cady Stanton and Lucretia Mott, brought together, for the first time, like-minded men and women with one agenda—women's rights. The convention accomplished a great deal, including the issuance of the Declaration of Sentiments.

> We hold these truths to be self-evident: that all men and women are created equal; that they are endowed by their Creator with certain inalienable rights; that among these are life, liberty, and the pursuit of happiness; that to secure these rights governments are instituted, deriving their just powers from the consent of the governed...
>
> The history of mankind is a history of repeated injuries and usurpations on the part of man toward woman, having in direct object the establishment of an absolute tyranny over her. To prove this, let facts be submitted to a candid world.
>
> He has never permitted her to exercise her inalienable right to the elective franchise. He has compelled her to submit to laws, in the formation of which she had no voice. He has withheld from her rights which are given to the most ignorant and degraded men—both natives and foreigners. Having deprived her of this first right of a citizen, the elective franchise, thereby leaving her without representation in the halls of legislation, he has oppressed her on all sides. He has made her, if married, in the eye of the law, civilly dead. He has taken from her all right in property, even to the wages she earns.

He has made her, morally, an irresponsible being, as she can commit many crimes, with impunity, provided they be done in the presence of her husband. In the covenant of marriage, she is compelled to promise obedience to her husband, he becoming, to all intents and purposes, her master—the law giving him power to deprive her of her liberty, and to administer chastisement.

He has so framed the laws of divorce, as to what shall be the proper causes of divorce; in case of separation, to whom the guardianship of the children shall be given, as to be wholly regardless of the happiness of women—the law, in all cases, going upon the false supposition of the supremacy of man, and giving all power into his hands.

After depriving her of all rights as a married woman, if single and the owner of property, he has taxed her to support a government which recognizes her only when her property can be made profitable to it.

He has monopolized nearly all the profitable employments, and from those she is permitted to follow, she receives but a scanty remuneration.

He closes against her all the avenues to wealth and distinction, which he considers most honorable to himself. As a teacher of theology, medicine, or law, she is not known.

He has denied her the facilities for obtaining a thorough education—all colleges being closed against her.

> He allows her in Church as well as State, but a subordinate position, claiming Apostolic authority for her exclusion from the ministry, and with some exceptions, from any public participation in the affairs of the Church.
>
> He has created a false sentiment, by giving to the world a different code of morals for men and women, by which moral delinquencies which exclude women from society, are not only tolerated but deemed of little account in man.
>
> He has usurped the prerogative of Jehovah himself, claiming it is his right to assign for her a sphere of action, when that belongs to her conscience and her God.
>
> He has endeavored, in every way that he could, to destroy her confidence in her own powers, to lessen her self-respect, and to make her willing to lead a dependent and abject life.[61]

Ironically, the delegates at the Seneca Falls Convention could not agree about the voting issue. Women voting was such a foreign idea that even these liberal-minded people could not conceive of it. It was not until Frederick Douglass, the famous African-American orator, spoke out in favor, saying that women and slaves had the right to be free, that some of the delegates agreed to support the suffrage movement.[62]

An important step had been taken in the signing of the Declaration of Sentiments at Seneca Falls. But the battle for women's rights had just begun. Step by step, women started to rise from their civil death. Still, 72 years would elapse before women would finally be granted the right to vote.

KEY WOMEN OF THE PERIOD

Emma Hart Willard (1787 - 1870)

> That the improvement of female education will be considered by our enlightened citizens as a subject of importance, the liberality with which they part with their property to educate their daughters is a sufficient evidence; and why should they not, when assembled in the Legislature, act in concert to effect a noble object which, though dear to them individually, cannot be accomplished by their unconnected exertions?

Emma Hart (later Emma Willard), perhaps the most famous of the early education reformers, is credited with being the first to make secondary education available for women. Hart was born in 1787 and began her teaching career at the age of 17. When she married a physician, John Willard, in 1809, she gave up teaching but continued her studies in private. Her nephew came to live with her while he was attending a nearby boys' academy, and as she read his books, she was astounded to discover the differences between the education provided to girls and boys. This revelation led her to draft a pamphlet called "A Plan for Female Education," which she sent to the governor of New York. The plan envisioned not only a charter for a seminary but a financial endowment to allow the operation of the school as well. The governor was so impressed with Willard's suggestions that he recommended the legislature appropriate money to establish a school that followed Willard's outline. Although the legislature voted her a charter for a seminary in Waterford, New York, no money was appropriated.

Some prominent citizens of Troy, New York (across the Hudson River from the capital city of Albany), were impressed by Willard's proposal and managed to raise money for a school building as well as funds for maintenance and staff. She moved to Troy and by 1821, the Troy Female Seminary became a reality and opened with 90 girls from seven states in attendance. The school has since been renamed in honor of Emma Willard and is today a college preparatory boarding and day school for girls in grades nine through twelve.

Considering that "learned young ladies" were deemed a liability in the marriage market, it is remarkable that Willard was able to transform the traditional mode of female education. How was she able to acquire the support she needed to implement her innovative ideas? Willard was an astute political strategist and a master of syllogistic logic. In presenting her arguments, she was very careful to play upon a popular theme that "educated" (and therefore intelligent) women were more likely to raise intelligent sons to become informed and patriotic citizens.

A dedicated educational reformer with respect to women's education, Willard was nevertheless careful to avoid mentioning, or even implying, that improved education might encourage women to think independently, or to be able to hold jobs outside the home. She did, however, make one exception about the value of outside work. She pointed to the advantages of educating women to become teachers who would then work for less than half the salary paid to male teachers. This argument found favor with cash-strapped school boards. An added advantage was that female teachers were expected to remain "spinsters" and devote their lives to their profession—without the distraction of a family. (This sacrifice was never expected of men.)

To gain support, she also used a rationale for women's education that did not require too much persuasion. She pointed out that teaching was a desirable profession for women since they were inherently more virtuous than men and, consequently, would exert their influence as teachers to uplift and purify American society. Willard's tactics, however skewed they may seem today, paved the way for women's secondary education.

Willard was a very accomplished person. A prolific writer on educational subjects, she also composed the inspirational hymn, "Rocked in the Cradle of the Deep." Additionally, she served as superintendent of schools for a Vermont town, worked with another education reformer to improve the public schools of Connecticut, and organized an association for the improvement of female teachers. By the time she retired in 1838, the Troy Female Seminary had educated several thousand students. Many of her former students went on to become successful educators themselves, and some founded seminaries of their own based on the Emma Willard model of education.[63]

Mary Lyon (1797-1849)

> It is one of the nicest of mental operations to distinguish between what is very difficult and what is utterly impossible.

Mary Lyon, best known as the founder of Mount Holyoke Female Seminary in 1837, was able to realize the impossible by obtaining an endowment for her seminary for girls. Lyon's observations of the experiences of other women who had founded schools convinced her that if she wanted her school to survive beyond her own lifetime she would need an endowment. Her major concern was that her school continue to offer education comparable in quality and cost to that offered men. There was good reason for her concern: The cost of a single year in a good quality girls' schools was often twice that of a man's entire college career. To raise money to permanently endow the school, Lyon needed to get her ideas before the public. There was, however, a calculated risk in "going public." It was considered improper for a woman to speak in public, soliciting funds for any cause, no matter how worthy.

Few people believed that Lyon would succeed in her ambition—after all, she believed that the sum of $27,000 needed to be raised to build and open the school. However, she was able to convince men—businessmen and ministers—to assume the responsibility of raising the funds. Unfortunately, public apathy combined with worsening economic conditions that resulted in the panic and depression of 1837, brought an end to the donations. Defying convention, Lyon took her green velvet bag and went out on her own to address meetings and solicit funds. When her friends remonstrated with her about her unladylike behavior, she replied: "Better to violate taste than not have the work done." She managed to raise over $27,000 from people in more than 92 towns. There were only two gifts as high as $1,000, and most of the donations ranged between six cents and five dollars.

The school opened on November 8, 1837, and even the small donors felt an ownership in the school they had helped to found. Mary Lyon lived only 12 years after her school opened. She was later commemorated for having established the first institution of its kind in the U.S.. Lyon, through opening and establishing Mount Holyoke, laid the foundation for the opening of Vassar in 1865, Smith and Wellesley in 1875, of the "Harvard Annex" in 1879, and of Bryn Mawr in 1885.[64]

Catharine Beecher (1800 – 1878)

> It appears then, that it is in America, alone, that women are raised to equality with the other sex; and that, both in theory and practice, their interests are regarded as of equal value.

Less famous than her sister, Harriet Beecher Stowe, who wrote *Uncle Tom's Cabin*, Catharine Beecher was an outstanding women's education reformer. Indeed, her contributions to the improvement of education for women entitles her to recognition as wide as her sister received. Born in 1800, Catherine Beecher began teaching school at age 19 to help her family financially. Her fiancée's untimely death in a shipwreck led her to decide to devote her life to service to others; she embarked on a teaching career.

In 1822, Beecher started a seminary for girls in Hartford, Connecticut, where her sister, Harriet, attended as a student, later becoming one of the assistant teachers. Poor health prohibited Beecher from keeping up the pace of running the school, and she was forced to resign in 1832. She moved to Cincinnati to be with her family and restore her health, but the local education reformers would not let her rest. She was pressured to start a school in their city, and so she did. After two years, she left the second school she had founded, and began to travel to Western states to survey educational systems.

The pamphlet that Beecher wrote to report her findings painted a dismal picture of the conditions she found. She noted that illiteracy was prevalent throughout the country. Schools were too few, and those that existed were poor in quality, dirty, overcrowded, and staffed by untrained teachers. On the basis of her findings, she concluded that 60,000 teachers would be needed within twelve years to teach the increasing numbers of the nation's children. She recommended that if the need were to be met, it would have to be from a pool of women teachers. Beecher's warning was realistic, as men found other callings more lucrative than teaching. She also criticized the lack of preparation required to be a teacher, pointing out that anyone could assume the position regardless of aptitude or training. Beecher told the government officials in each town she visited that even a shoemaker required an apprenticeship, and a nine-year course was required to make young men good preachers.

Beecher made many changes in the schools she was associated with, based on her analysis of the improvements required to upgrade the quality of education. For example, she introduced calisthenics in a course of physical education and later her writings did much to introduce domestic science into the American school curriculum. She also used many visual aids such as maps and apparatuses. Significantly, many of these changes are incorporated into the teaching methods currently in use. Unfortunately neither her success nor her reputation as an educator led to what she desired most: to have her school endowed. It was not until after her death that one of the schools she founded obtained an endowment. Catherine Beecher was not alone in being denied the opportunity to perpetuate her school. It was much more difficult during this period to get a girls' school incorporated (to have a charter issued) or endowed (permanent funding established) than it was a boys' school. It was not until 1873 that the perpetuity of Emma Willard's school was assured.[65]

Prudence Crandall (1803 – 1890)

> My feelings began to awaken. I saw the prejudice of the whites against color was deep and inveterate. In my humble opinion, it was the strongest, if not the only chain that bound those heavy burdens on the wretched slaves.... I contemplated that for a while, the manner in which I might best serve the people of color. As wealth was not mine, I saw no means of benefiting them, than by imparting to those of my own sex that were anxious to learn, all the instruction I might be able to give however small the amount.

Prudence Crandall was a Quaker who ran a successful seminary for young ladies in Centerbury, Connecticut. In 1833, her servant—a free African-American woman—persuaded her to accept a young African-American girl, Sarah Harris, into her school of "sheltered and proper" young ladies. The Caucasian parents objected, so rather than oust her new pupil, Crandall decided to close her school. Two months after she closed her "proper" school, she opened another with 17 African-American pupils in attendance.

It would not be difficult to imagine how this second affront was taken by the people in the community. The men threatened her, and when this failed, they resorted to more overt tactics. They even tried to jail Crandall on a vagrancy charge. When the charge failed to stand up in court, her persecutors petitioned for a special law to the Connecticut legislature making it illegal to teach a pupil from another state. When this action failed, they turned to time-honored scare tactics used by mobs to intimidate their targets. They broke windows, threw rocks at the teachers and students, and dropped debris in her well. Local storekeepers refused to sell her food, and doctors in the community denied her and her students medical attention.

Crandall and her students withstood the pressure for over a year, and the school became a symbol of equal rights. Supporters brought food and sent funds, and her own father carted water for the school from his well over two miles away. As each act of terror failed, the next set became even more violent. The perpetrators finally resorted to setting fire to the building and using battering rams to demolish the interior. The destruction forced Crandall to admit defeat, fearing for the lives of her students. Her tormentors succeeded in driving her out, but their violent actions did not daunt her spirit. Her courage in the face of grave danger has not been forgotten. Today, in belated gratitude, a woman's dormitory at Howard University in Washington, D.C., bears the name "Crandall Hall."

Crandall's heroics in the face of impossible odds are all the more remarkable when viewed within the context of the day. At the time she started her school for young African-American girls, Mount Holyoke was not yet a reality, and the voices of the many women who later would speak publicly against the institution of slavery had not yet been raised. Significantly, no one followed in her footsteps for some 20 years.[66]

Sarah Grimkë (1792-1873) and Angelina Grimkë Weld (1805-1879)

> What, then, can woman do for the slave, when she herself is under the feet of man and shamed into silence?

By the 1830s, women were actively involved in the growing abolition movement and, eventually realizing the many parallels between the rights denied slaves and the rights denied women, the women's rights movement. Women's involvement in improving their condition in life was sparked by the actions of the Grimkë sisters—Sarah and Angelina. Although having been raised by a wealthy and aristocratic slave-owning family in Charleston, South Carolina, the sisters were outspoken in their opposition to slavery and moved to the North, joining the Quaker movement. In 1835, Angelina wrote a letter that was published in the abolitionist newspaper, *The Liberator.*

The Grimkë sisters then embarked on careers as abolitionist speakers and writers, but they also had another agenda. They were committed to bringing before the public their views opposing the existing order of "proper female behavior." As they began to attract larger and larger audiences apparently equally willing to entertain ideas about both issues, their abolitionist sponsors became alarmed. They feared that the introduction of the taboo topic of women's rights would detract from what they perceived as the more legitimate one of abolition.

The male abolitionists were not the only ones who were alarmed about this radical tendency to spread the word about women's rights. Catharine Beecher publicly expressed her disapproval of the controversial ideas being advanced by the Grimkës. Beecher was opposed to displacing the basic Victorian principles of "true womanhood." She made it clear during her pioneering work to improve women's education that her sole purpose was to help women carry out their true mission as wives and mothers. Beecher was equally opposed to what she felt was "radical abolitionism," preferring "gradualism" and even "colonization" for African Americans as a more accepted remedy. She was adamantly opposed to females taking an active role in the abolitionist movement and opposed the feminist movement in all its forms.

Angelina Grimkë was incensed by Beecher's stand, and replied to her in a series of letters, later reprinted in book form. In her letters, which she made public, she defended abolitionist theories and attacked the idea of colonization for African Americans. She also defended the right of women to act as full-fledged citizens. Not surprisingly, the sisters' bold stand on vital social issues commanded a great deal of unfavorable attention during a period when women were supposed to be neither seen nor heard.[67]

Chapter Two
Preparing to Fight

Overview

There was very little about the nineteenth century to encourage the start of an organized women's movement. Opposition was diverse, powerful and rampant. Historians and political scientists offer several different interpretations for how a cultural phenomenon of this magnitude could take place in a century when women were, perhaps, more repressed than at any other time. The explanations point to other historical occurrences such as the rise of industrialization, rebellion against the restrictive Victorian society mores, the impact of the "age of enlightenment," fallout from the idea of freedom emanating from the American Revolution, and the movement to abolish slavery. It is not clear why the women's rights movement began; it is clear, however, that it began to gain crucial momentum.[1]

The period between the 1840s and the 1860s has been called the Age of Reform. The most sought after reform for women was getting the vote. It is important to note, however, that the suffrage movement was only one of many other reform movements going on at the time that involved women. A struggle for equal rights for women consumed the time and attention of many activists (some of the suffragettes were strongly opposed to equal rights). Other female activists focused solely on abolition, or improving women's educational opportunities, or paving the way for women to enter the professions. Some believed that the only reason the vote was necessary was so that women would have the clout to clean up the immorality of the American people—i.e., American men. Conversely, some of the women who fought for equal rights did not deem it necessary to vote, and concentrated their energy on legal issues such as reforming divorce laws, gaining property rights for women, and obtaining equity in employment. The different priorities and beliefs resulted in conflict between factions, diverting the ultimate strength of the women's rights movement for years.[2]

After the Declaration of Sentiments

The Seneca Falls Convention in 1848 signaled the dawning of a new day for organized reform movements. There were no follow-up sessions to Seneca Falls specifically, but until the Civil War, a women's rights convention was conducted somewhere in the United States nearly very year. The women who attended these conventions found ways to put their beliefs into action. Activists in various states began petitioning their state legislatures to grant married women legal rights. By 1860, they began to see results from their hard work. States began to confer legal status on women to own property and be able to control their own earnings.[3]

Voting rights for women was a controversial issue at Seneca Falls, and was not seriously addressed in the women's rights movement until much later. Seneca Falls activists were devoted to bringing women's issues before the public to increase the number of supporters. This effort was successful in attracting a growing number of women and men, who began to show support through financial donations and active participation. Nonetheless, the increase in numbers was not sufficient to become the viable political force that the leaders had hoped it would be.

It is not clear how extensive the involvement of professional women was in the various women's movements.[4] However, there is evidence that many professional women supported the idea that women were the equal of men in every way. They publicly advocated that any social or political constraints that interfered with gaining the equality women were entitled to should be changed or abolished. Their numbers, in total, however, in the mid-nineteenth century were quite small. By 1910, there were estimated to be 1,500 female lawyers nationwide and 9,000 women doctors.[5] Although women categorized as professionals constituted 11.9% of the women in the work force by 1920, 75% of these individuals were nurses or teachers.[6]

Equal access to the professions was important enough to the early activists to be included in resolutions associated with the Declaration of Sentiments:

> Resolved, that the speedy success of our cause depends upon the zealous and untiring efforts of both men and women, for the overthrow of the monopoly of the pulpit, and for the securing to women an equal participation with men in the various trades, professions, and commerce.[7]

After The Civil War

> All persons born or naturalized in the United States, and subject to the jurisdiction thereof, are citizens of the United States and of the State wherein they reside. No State shall make or enforce any law which shall abridge the privileges or immunities of citizens of the United States; nor shall any State deprive any person of life, liberty, or property, without due process of law; nor deny to any person within its jurisdiction the equal protection of the laws.
>
> — Fourteenth Amendment, U.S. Constitution
> (Ratified July 9, 1868)

> The right of citizens of the United States to vote shall not be denied or abridged by the United States or by

any state on account of race, color, or previous condition of servitude.

— Fifteenth Amendment, U.S. Constitution
(Ratified February 3, 1870)[8]

Most historians agree that the Civil War was not about slavery per se; it was about economics and the rights of states—slavery was only a factor. Racism, discrimination, and unequal rights did not end with the Emancipation Proclamation in 1862, the surrender in Appomatox in 1865, or the passage of both Fourteenth and Fifteenth Amendments to the U.S. Constitution; the uphill struggle for equality was to continue for generations to come. Gaining freedom did not entitle freed African-American men to all of the privileges of full citizenship. The coveted right to vote for example, didn't occur until almost five years after slavery was abolished—when the Fifteenth Amendment was ratified. Even after ratification, ways were found to disenfranchise African Americans in the South.

When the Civil War broke out in 1860, it ended the first stage of the women's rights movement. The women's rights leaders' expectations for their own cause after the war ended were to be frustrated. Having set aside their own demands during the war to devote themselves to patriotic causes, they naively assumed that a grateful government would reward them for their efforts. Mostly they counted on the backing of the Republicans who already had their eyes on enlarging the electorate by a potential windfall of 2 million male African-American voters. Women calculated that their own enfranchisement would add immeasurably to the Republican's expected windfall. Their expectations, however, for support from the federal government were disappointed, and they were ill-prepared for the resistance that came from the politicians. Republicans, it turns out, had no intention of jeopardizing their chances to land the influx of African-American male voters by supporting the still damaging issue of women's suffrage. Additionally, Republicans were not sure they could control women once they had the right to vote, whereas they thought could control a newly enfranchised African-American minority.[9]

Women were disappointed by supposed allies as well. Those male abolitionists who had not already deserted them backed down after the war and withdrew their support. They justified their withdrawal by saying that this was the "Blacks' hour," and nothing should be allowed to interfere with its success. In 1866, suffragettes discovered that the word "male" would be used in three different locations in the second section of the Fourteenth Amendment, if adopted as proposed.[10]

Feminist leaders Susan B. Anthony, Elizabeth Cady Stanton, and Lucy Stone were understandably crushed by the news that women had been left out of the proposed Constitutional amendment. It meant that their struggle was far from over, and yet another amendment would be required to give women the vote in federal elections. Stanton predicted that the movement would be set back a full century. Anthony and Stanton were so angry, they railed against the "Black race and foreigners" rather than against the white male politicians who were the ones responsible for shattering their dreams. Anthony made a pledge she would rather cut off her right arm before she would work to demand the ballot for the "Black" and not the woman. Stanton made derogatory references to "Sambo," and blasted a policy that would permit the enfranchisement of foreigners—many of whom could neither speak nor write English—the moment they touched foot on American soil.[11]

The Fourteenth Amendment to the Constitution was ratified in July 1868. While it guaranteed civil rights, its language was not strong enough to satisfy the radical Republicans that the African-American freed men would have the right to vote. As a consequence, a Fifteenth Amendment was introduced to address this situation. Stanton and Anthony argued that the Fifteenth Amendment should have included the word "sex," but it did not.[12]

The women experienced another major disappointment, which came from Frederick Douglass, the influential African-American orator who had passionately supported Stanton's plea for women's suffrage at Seneca Falls. He reversed his position in 1869 and threw his entire support behind securing the vote for African Americans. He made his position clear by drawing a distinction between the plight of the freedmen in the South and that of women. When asked by an individual in the audience if the deplorable conditions did not also apply to African-American women, he unhesitatingly replied that although this was true, it was not because of being a woman but because of being African American.[13]

Lucy Stone was disappointed by the turn of events, but she took a different tack than either Anthony or Stanton. She urged that the wording of the proposed amendment be changed to reflect enfranchisement of women. She added if these changes were not possible, she favored its passage anyway, because as she explained, "I will be thankful in my soul if anybody can get out of this terrible pit."[14]

Some historians point out that Anthony, Stanton, and others had reason to respond with anger. They believed that the "Blacks' hour" could have been the "women's hour" as well. Their optimistic hope of linking the two issues was an example of political naiveté. They could not accept that two simultaneous radical moves were outside the realm of practical political reality and that slavery and the condition of the African Americans had been a large national issue for many years, leading to a civil war. A tremendous amount of work was still to be done before the general public, and the politicians who represented them, would consider women's suffrage as important an issue as African-American suffrage.[15]

The Dawning of Universal Education

> Only an entirely unwomanly young woman could try to become so thoroughly learned, in a man's sense of the term; and she would try in vain, for she has not the mental faculties of a man.
>
> Author unknown[16]

Starting in the mid-nineteenth century, education for women became more of a reality for the masses. Education was not the imperative for the general population in the 1800s that it is in the early 2000s, and thus was not seen as necessary or even desirable for women. Early in the 1800s, the private seminaries and academies provided an education for female students whose families were interested in having their daughters educated and who could afford the fees. For more females to be educated, the public school system needed to be expanded. This was, indeed, a formidable task. It took the better part of the nineteenth century to expand the free education system for males from elementary schools through high school. By 1860, there were only about 40 schools that qualified as high schools in the entire country. Many others, which called themselves high schools, were little better than elementary schools.[17]

Not surprisingly, the effort to obtain free education for girls progressed even more slowly. Education at the elementary level (basic reading, writing and arithmetic) was open to girls, but admission into secondary schools was not. It was not until Emma Willard started her school for girls in 1821, and Mount Holyoke Seminary was founded in 1837, that females gained the opportunity for an academically rigorous secondary education.[18]

In the mid-nineteenth century, the United States led the rest of the world in the amount of public and private education available to females. College education became available for women starting in 1837, at Oberlin College. Some of the early seminaries advertised themselves as "women colleges," although they hardly qualified for this distinction. Their academic standards did not compare to the quality of education offered to young men at Harvard College and other Eastern all-male institutions. Troy Seminary and Mount Holyoke came closest to offering a semblance of higher education; however, their major contribution was to prepare their students for a successful college experience.

The Oberlin experience gave women the opportunity to demonstrate that they were equal to the challenge of performing academically at the higher education level. Their academic excellence became a convincing argument that investment in women's education was worth the cost, as well as the risk. The battle for gender equality in higher education was not yet over, but the way had been cleared for the opening of Antioch in 1852, Vassar in 1865, Smith and Wellesley in 1875, and Bryn Mawr in 1885. Also during this period, many other chartered women colleges were established, leaving critics to wonder where it would all end. To the dismay of many, this rash of women's colleges was only the beginning of women's ambitions in higher education.[19]

An important point to bear in mind is that even the best men's colleges during this period would not shine according to today's standards. Requirements for education at the levels needed today for professional careers, including graduate school, did not exist.[20]

Even the big three at the time—Harvard, Princeton, and Yale—were no better than present-day high schools. Harvard was poverty-stricken and struggling to keep its doors open. Yale's facilities were even more insufficient and its curriculum antiquated, as was Princeton's. As inadequate as these institutions were, they still were superior to most education provided to women until the women's colleges opened their doors. The new women's colleges were determined to bridge the gap by providing opportunity and setting high scholastic standards.[21]

Women's Education Blooms

The four decades following the Civil War saw a dramatic expansion of higher education for women. There had been pressure from the growing feminist movement in the East but, primarily, the motive for relaxing barriers against female admission was based on dire financial need. The all-male institutions faced decreased enrollments as an aftermath of the war, economic depression, and student dissatisfaction with the courses offered. In the West, most institutions of higher learning were already state supported and usually coeducational from the time of their founding because males were not enrolled in sufficient numbers to support them otherwise, and taxpayers would not support the institutions unless their daughters could enroll.[22]

By 1870, Wisconsin, Michigan, Missouri, Iowa, Kansas, Indiana, Minnesota, and California had established coeducational state universities. This liberalization of policy did not represent a change of heart concerning a woman's proper sphere, but was dictated by politics and finances. Educational institutions continued to educate women for marriage and appropriate female jobs, such as public school teaching. The college experience intentionally was designed to discourage women from engaging in independent thought or pursuing careers in "masculine" fields.[23]

The influx of women into higher education spawned age-old arguments about women's limitations—most notably, an alleged lack of the physical and mental capacity necessary to absorb and use higher-order learning. Many argued (until recently actually) that women with college degrees were less likely to marry than those who did not attend college. Despite the absence of proof, many families discouraged their daughters from seeking a college education, fearing they would become "spinsters." Still, the number of women going to college increased dramatically between 1860 and 1920, as educational opportunities became available and as women saw the economic and personal benefits of becoming educated. By the 1900s, over 47 percent of the total college enrollment was female—a testament, perhaps, to women's growing understanding that education was one important key to progress.[24]

Education for Ethnic Minorities

The opening of education for women in general coincided with a gradual loosening of walls barring minorities from attaining education. Educational opportunities had been made available to Native Americans by the federal government when their support was needed after the Revolutionary War. The idea was to teach Native Americans useful skills such as settled farming and Christianity, and in many ways, constituted forced assimilation.[25]

African Americans experienced a different set of problems in their quest for education before and after emancipation. Prior to the Civil War, most African-American men and women were either slaves in the South, or oppressed because of their race in the North. It was illegal to educate slaves in the Southern states, and African-American children were banned from attending school in many non-slave states and territories.[26] Plantation owners occasionally provided the bare essentials of training to enable their plantations to function more efficiently. However, the general practice was to forbid slaves from being educated for fear they might seek ways to escape their bondage. Most education was provided by Quakers, who also were abolitionists, and by African-American "freedmen," who helped to educate other African Americans at great personal risk to themselves.

Before emancipation, abolitionists and religious groups attempted to break down the barriers to education for African Americans and beseeched other Caucasian Americans to join their cause. They were not successful in breaking through either public opposition or apathy. Consequently, their efforts were largely fragmented, and did not achieve the desired results of increasing the literacy rate of newly freed African Americans (male or female) after emancipation.[27]

Entering the Professions

By 1920, only about 12 percent of working women worked in professions that required education past high school. Seventy-five percent of those who were professionals held jobs in the traditionally female professions of nursing and teaching. The so-called "learned professions," or "higher professions," those requiring advanced levels of education, scarcely had any female representation.[28] For women aspiring to professional careers, the right to higher education was crucial. The much-coveted doctorate, for example, was not even offered at women's colleges until late in the nineteenth century, and many institutions did not offer women a doctorate until well into the twentieth century.[29]

American graduate institutions that offered doctorates strongly resisted admitting women, at least partly because of the model on which these institutions were based—German universities, which admitted only men.

Overcoming resistance to offering women graduate education was a three-stage process that involved aggressive action and perseverance by the women's education pioneers. Before 1890, women had gained very little in terms of graduate training. When finally admitted, they were described as "special students" and were allowed in graduate programs at only six major graduate schools. To top it off, they were not allowed to matriculate. Their protests against this unfair situation went unheeded. These policies remained in effect for many years, with the result that women were denied the right to earn their degrees—even when they met or exceeded all of the requirements.[30]

Why didn't the women's colleges offer an alternative to the all-male colleges with their entrenched discriminatory policies against female graduate students? Most of the women's institutions had been successful at instituting high standards at the undergraduate level. However, many women's colleges lacked sufficient financial resources to institute graduate programs. Similar to their predecessors—the female seminaries—they found it difficult to become endowed to the same extent as the all-male institutions. As a result, they lacked sufficient funds to build adequate graduate facilities and laboratories or to recruit qualified faculty to conduct the courses.[31]

Even if the necessary resources had been available, neither the students nor the female professors favored a segregated experience at the graduate level. Graduating from a prestigious coeducational school was an important career move for a woman. Consequently, women's colleges were unlikely to attract a sufficient number of students in each specialty to justify the cost of implementing graduate programs.[32]

Few doctoral programs were offered and maintained at the women's colleges, although Bryn Mawr was an exception, due to the efforts of its dean and later president M. Carey Thomas. Mount Holyoke, Wellesley and Smith were able to establish a limited number of master's degree programs. For most of the women's colleges, however, the obstacles to installing graduate programs were so formidable that they did not attempt to establish master's or doctoral programs. And as these were not accessible to women at the men's institutions, it seemed that the doctorate would be forever denied women. Fortunately, a few courageous women were determined to reverse this fate.[33]

Change was inevitable, and eventually, coeducation at both the undergraduate and graduate levels became a fact at many of the all-male institutions. By 1900, many of the universities in the U.S. had succumbed to the pressure and had begun to accept women and award them doctorates. During the process of integration, some schools began admitting women to the graduate school before its doors opened to female undergraduates. Yale University, for example, admitted female graduate students in 1891, but refused to accept them at the undergraduate level.[34]

As women's applications to graduate and professional schools increased at what some men perceived as an alarming rate, many of the coeducation schools reversed their "open-door" policies. Some of the "prestigious" men's colleges vowed to never open their doors at all to women, particularly the doors to their professional schools. Johns Hopkins did not award women doctorates until 1907, 31 years after the school opened, and 15 years after it had admitted women to its medical school. Harvard evaded the issue by forming the Radcliffe Graduate school in 1902 for women. In addition, Harvard did not admit women to its medical school until 1945, its law school until 1950, and its business school until 1963.[35] And Columbia University did not admit women into its undergraduate program until 1985.

Backlash to Women Professionals

As women began to enter the professions, a backlash developed among the men. As increasing numbers of women sought higher education and professional training, these women appeared to loom as competition in fields that men felt were overcrowded already. Men also feared that the status of those professions women entered would be lowered.

Although it appears that so-called "professionalization" may not have been strictly aimed at women and minorities, its impact was felt more significantly as women and minorities entered the "learned" fields—the professions—in the late nineteenth century. New professional standards were laid down, hinging on education and certification requirements. As a result of these requirements, both college and professional training became the prerequisites for admission to the bar, licensing of physicians, and membership in professional societies. In many instances, higher membership requirements were foisted on women for admission to professional societies, and even with higher qualifications, they were restricted to lower levels of membership. The process was instrumental in excluding large numbers of women from professional fields for the greater part of the nineteenth century.[36]

Minority Women's Education

The great majority of the progress that was made in higher education for women affected only white women. Education for female minorities improved during this period, but was nowhere near the level of white women's education which, of course, was nowhere near the level of white men's education. However, the idea that higher education could uplift minority races took hold with both white and African American educators toward the end of the nineteenth century. During the period between 1875 and 1920, the development of single-sex colleges for African-American women and for white women had increased. There were, however, differences between the kinds of training made available for each race. The prestigious schools for white women, commonly called "The Seven Sisters," were determined to provide an education for their students equal to that of the men's Ivy League colleges. In some cases, the women's schools were even more experimental than the men's institutions, especially in their science curriculum. The women colleges created innovative laboratory research and pioneered in developing new social science courses as well.[37]

In contrast, the trend for African-American women's and men's colleges was to move toward vocational education. This trend was largely influenced by Booker T. Washington, who founded Tuskegee Institute in 1881 as the Normal School for Negroes, on the premise that every graduate should master basic academic disciplines and a marketable trade.[38]

Washington was a firm believer that vocational training would provide African Americans with a market advantage that they lacked. W.E.B. Dubois, a prominent and influential orator of the time, rejected this argument, calling it "accommodation." He believed that vocational training would create a new, lower occupational class for African Americans. He wanted to see African Americans have the opportunity for a liberal arts education.[39]

Washington's pragmatic approach eventually won, and many of the African-American women's colleges developed vocational programs as well. The home economics curricula became popular. One all African-American college, Spelman College, did not follow this trend. The college was founded by two white women, Sophie Packard and Harriet Giles, both from strong New England abolitionist backgrounds. Packard and Giles decided to offer both liberal arts and technical skills in the school's curricula to give students a choice of which path to follow.[40]

In the nineteenth century, minority education was not as rigidly divided along gender lines. Many African-American women were educated in coeducational institutions. A few single-sex colleges were opened for African-American women during the pioneer period, all located in the South. Bennett College was founded in Greensboro, North Carolina, in 1873, as a coeducational institution, but later was converted into a liberal arts college for African-American women. Two other colleges for African-American women were founded during this period: Barber-Scotia in Concord, North Carolina, in 1867, and Houston Tillotson in Austin, Texas, in 1876. Despite the increase in access to higher education, by 1890, only 30 African-American women held college degrees.[41]

For both Native Americans and African Americans, lack of educational opportunities remained a major barrier to economic and social development. Few women of either ethnic group attained professional status during the first decades of the twentieth century. Mexican-American women, many of whom had settled the Southwest and California long before the Mayflower landed, could not even dream of careers. Before and after the U.S.-Mexico War in 1846-1848, Mexican Americans lost their lands and their rights. Latinos became an invisible minority for many decades thereafter.

In spite of the many obstacles placed in their way, women did strive for and obtain the education and other qualifications necessary to enter the professions. Most visibly, they entered the medical and legal fields. Less visibly, they entered fields like accounting, the sciences, and the academic realm. Finally, women even entered engineering, although their numbers and percentage in this field today remains the lowest of any of the professions. As women entered the medical and legal professions in the 1800s and early 1900s, their attention was focused not only on their work, but also on the women's rights movement.

Women in Medicine Take One Step at a Time

The feminist movement was the crucial instrument of progress for nineteenth-century medical women. The reason some women might have been opposed to it is that they were resigned to the fact they lacked any real power in medical institutions. They could do little more than protest the unfairness of their treatment, and never possessed sufficient political clout to influence policy changes. Despite the detractors among the ranks, the women's rights movement was a cause to which some of the nineteenth-century women doctors were deeply committed, and even served in leadership positions.[42]

The earlier women medical pioneers had managed to combat each problem they faced with a single solution, and were able to forge ahead by taking one step at a time. Their legacy, however, was not to be lasting change. Their ongoing battle to achieve equity in their profession had to be resumed by successive generations of women in medicine that followed them.

Women in Law Make a Difference

Female lawyers have been around only as long as the nineteenth century women's rights movement. Not surprisingly, women lawyers were at the forefront of the fight for equal rights and did not hesitate to use their legal skills on behalf of advancing women's causes. Women lawyers had a compelling motive for their dedication to legal reform movements; they had been discriminated against in their profession from the start and were denied access to the bar until after the Civil War. The laws prohibiting women from practicing law eliminated them from competition with men in a prestigious and well-paid occupation. These barriers remained in place for several decades after lawyer Myra Bradwell filed the first sex discrimination case ever to be heard by the U.S. Supreme Court, in 1870.

Many women became lawyers in order to improve the condition of those who were less fortunate than themselves—particularly less fortunate women. For many of these women who were socially conscious, it was an easy transition from working in their often less than lucrative practices to spearheading campaigns for child custody and divorce law reform. They also tended to help indigent women, who had few legal alternatives.

Many of these early women lawyers also became activists in the temperance movement, seeing a connection between gaining the right to vote and prohibition. Under the "Laws of Coverture," married women were not entitled to keep their own earnings, even if the money was necessary to support the family. An alcoholic husband, therefore, had the right to confiscate and spend any wages his wife earned. With no welfare system in place to provide assistance to a destitute family, the wife and children of an alcoholic were subject to the most abject poverty. A common argument against reforming this situation was that there were orphanages and institutions available for poor people.

Drinking was considered a "manly art." To deny men this privilege was unthinkable and for many years not taken seriously. Some women lawyers had first-hand experience with the helplessness of a family totally dependent upon the whims of an alcoholic husband. They felt that the reform urgently needed for the salvation of families made destitute by drinking would not be possible without women acquiring the right to vote. Once the connection between reform and political power was made, women lawyers began working hard for women's suffrage by using their "legal" wiles.

The efforts by Bradwell and other women lawyers, in conjunction with the women's rights movement, destroyed many barriers so that by the end of the nineteenth century, women lawyers were practicing in almost every state in the Union. However, by today's standards, there were so few of these practitioners that they were only tokens. It is important to note that these victories had been accomplished on a state-by-state basis. Most realized that broader-based change would require national legislation.[43]

Women in all the professions benefited greatly from the many legal reforms enacted in the early 1900s. The number of women employed in the professions expanded dramatically by the beginning of the twentieth century—about the same time the suffragist movement was getting into full swing. The surge of women into the work force provided fresh arguments to support the need for suffrage, and many of the newly working women joined the ranks of the suffragists.

KEY WOMEN OF THIS PERIOD

Myrtilla Miner (1815 – 1864)

> ...There is no law to prevent my teaching these people, and I shall teach them, even unto death.

The education of African-American girls had progressed little in the almost 20 years since Prudence Crandall ran her girls' school against all odds. Even in the North, African-American girls were barred from most schools, except those taught by other African Americans, who usually lacked the necessary training. Then along came Myrtilla Miner, who launched a one-woman campaign to open a school to prepare young

African-American women for teaching careers. Her struggle was vigorous and significant, although not well known today.

Born in 1815, Miner grew up in a tiny village in central New York. Although she wanted an education desperately, her family was very poor, so her dreams seemed hopeless. At one point, she wrote to the governor of New York, who gave her vague encouragement, but little else. She finally was admitted to an integrated Quaker seminary in Rochester, New York. While there, she became friends with two African-American students who told her about slavery. She learned even more about it when, after leaving the school, she became a teacher in a school for planters' daughters in Mississippi. Quite innocently, she asked to teach the slave children on the plantation as well, and was astounded when she was refused.

Miner was so moved by this experience that she came back North with a strong resolution to open a school for young African-American women. She chose Washington, D.C. because "it was the common property of the nation." Little did she realize that the political climate in the nation's capital before the Civil War was no better than in other parts of the country. Educating African Americans was not a popular issue—particularly African-American women—as they were the major source of domestic help in white households.

Many of Miner's associates tried to discourage her from this risky venture. Even Frederick Douglass, the great African-American educator and orator, did his best to dissuade her from this move as he envisioned her being in great physical danger if she pursued her plans. His arguments had no effect on what he called her "heroic spirit." In autumn 1851, Miner opened her school with six pupils. She faced the same sort of mob mentality as Crandall had faced 18 years prior. Unafraid, she challenged her detractors, saying that if they tore down her house she would simply get another. She would not permit anything to prevent her from carrying out her mission. Fortunately, she had some moral and financial support on her side. Harriet Beecher Stowe, for one, gave $1,000 of her royalties from *Uncle Tom's Cabin*; other Quakers and abolitionists gave money and donated time to the school.

Miner was responsible for keeping the school afloat from day-to-day. Along with her administrative and teaching duties, she lobbied congressmen, pressured journalists for publicity and solicited funds from the public. Unfortunately, this lifestyle was so taxing that by 1859, at age 44, she was forced to close the school because of ill health.

While at the helm of her school, Miner created three departments: primary teaching, domestic economy, and teacher training. She left a legacy of her courageous work on behalf of African-American females who otherwise would have had no public opportunity to become educated.

Myrtilla Miner died in 1864 in a horseback riding accident, when she was 49 years old. But her dream had been fulfilled. Miner Teachers College graduated many teachers over the years and later became a part of the District of Columbia Teachers College.[44]

Ellen Henrietta Swallow Richards (1842 – 1911)

> Perhaps the fact that I am not a Radical or a believer in the all powerful ballot for women to right her wrongs and that I do not scorn womanly duties, but claim it is a privilege to clean up and supervise the room and sew things, etc., is winning me stronger allies than anything else.

Ellen Henrietta Swallow Richards took a conservative approach to redressing educational inequities for women. Although it was apparent to her that every effort was being made to shut women out of the traditionally all-male professions, she concluded, "If women were not to be let in, why struggle?" The way around this barrier was to create a new profession that would not be competitive with men. This non-threatening approach would give women the advantage of a higher education and provide a path to enable them to teach in institutions of higher learning.

Richards almost single-handedly created the field of home economics, or "domestic science," as it was also called. In the period between 1880 and 1910, she devoted her entire career to establishing and promoting this "new profession for women." She ran demonstration projects, showcasing its merits, wrote training guides, and trained the first wave of banner carriers. In some circles, she was roundly applauded for her contribution to women's curricula in higher education; in others, she was denounced publicly by critics for the harm she was doing to the women's rights movement.

The main criticism was that "domestic science" was not science at all, but rather a thinly disguised attempt to elevate the status of menial household chores. Critics claimed that the introduction of a program of this nature into college curricula would support the view that women were only capable of doing "women's work." Considering Richards was herself a chemist, it is not likely her intention was to promote "women's work." More likely, she intended to open another door of opportunity for women.

Richards herself suffered disappointments in education. She was thwarted in her effort to be awarded a doctorate after completing the requirements. M.I.T. refused to award her the Ph.D. because she was the first chemistry Ph.D. that the school had ever had—and officials did not want that honor going to a woman.

Despite the criticism surrounding home economics, within a few decades, over 200 colleges had established home economics degree programs. Most of the more prestigious women's colleges did not join in the movement, but the course found favor with the coeducation schools, particularly the new land grant and agricultural colleges. For these schools, the new "all female" program served a dual purpose of satisfying the demand for more technical training and it effectively sidetracked women into a non-masculine professional career that did not compete with men.[45]

Christine Ladd-Franklin (1847 – 1930)

> There is certainly a crying need for all the psychologists who have any logic in them to pull well together and to put up a good fight against all the irrational cranks!... Is this then a good time, my dear Professor Titchener, for you to hold to the mediaeval attitude of not admitting me to your coming psychological conference in New York—at my very door? So unconscientious, so immortal—worse than that—so unscientific!

Christine Ladd-Franklin was one of the education pioneers of the late nineteenth century who laid the groundwork for women's graduate education. Ladd-Franklin chose the radical, direct frontal attack—never apologetic, and never backing down from a challenge. Her contributions were quite visible and were the subject of wide debate. Her main goal was to prod universities to open their doors to women for graduate training and for women to be granted the degrees that they had earned.

Ladd-Franklin vigorously fought her battles with universities across two continents for several decades. She never hesitated to use any weapon in her considerable arsenal to achieve her objectives, and was known for being very resourceful. When she needed it, she called on the support of the newly formed Association of Collegiate Alumnae—and got it! When she needed funds, she solicited financial backing from wealthy women—and got it! Ladd-Franklin was successful in achieving nearly every objective but one: her Ph.D.

Ladd-Franklin was strongly motivated by her personal experience of rejection by Johns Hopkins University. In 1878, she was accepted into the graduate program as a "special student." After successfully completing all the requirements for a doctoral degree, school officials refused to award her the doctorate. Indeed, it was not until she was 79 years old—44 years later—that what the school later called a "grievous wrong" was rectified.

Ladd-Franklin did not waste her time sulking over the slight she had received. She knew educational injustices would continue unless something was done. Recognizing the complexity of the issue, she decided that she needed to address policies that refused admission to women as well as the equally abhorrent policy of not granting women the degrees they had earned. Fortunately, Ladd-Franklin was not alone in fighting these battles—there were other equally determined women willing to join her. Ladd-Franklin was always the one in front leading the fight, and encouraging others when they became discouraged. Eventually, she was successful in achieving policy changes.[46]

Key Women Doctors

> The purpose of the women's medical movement is for occupying positions which men can not fully occupy and exercising an influence which men can not wield at all.
> —Dr. Elizabeth Blackwell

Dr. Harriot Hunt is credited with being the first woman to establish a successful medical practice in America. She and her sister, Sarah, started their own practice in Boston in 1835. However, they had to stop making house calls and eventually restricted their practice to women and children. She was the first woman to apply to, and be rejected by, Harvard Medical College. In 1847, the dean agreed to allow her to attend lectures not for credit, but the students submitted resolutions to the faculty that led to the denial of her request. Women were not admitted to the Harvard medical college until 1945. The only medical degree that she was ever to possess was an honorary one granted by the Female Medical College of Pennsylvania in 1853. Her efforts to obtain a formal medical education was the opening round of women's struggles to become full-fledged medical professionals.

Ann Preston had been rejected by several medical schools after having served an apprenticeship with a Quaker doctor. In 1842, she contacted a group of Quaker physicians, all of whom were frustrated with efforts to find colleges willing to accept their female apprentices. By 1850, the Female Medical College of Pennsylvania became the first chartered medical school for women. Although the state medical society resolved to expel any member who taught at the new school or helped out its faculty, six male physicians taught the first class of 40 women. The College closely briefly during the Civil War and then reopened as the Women's Medical College of Philadelphia. In 1970, it became a coeducational institution and was renamed the Medical College of Pennsylvania.

Dr. Elizabeth Blackwell became, in January 1849, the first woman in the U.S. to graduate from medical school (where she graduated first in her class) and the first woman doctor of medicine in modern times. Her medical education was not without drama, however. Blackwell applied to many medical schools, most of which did not even respond to her request for admission. However, her application was accompanied by a strong letter of recommendation from the Quaker doctor with whom she worked. When she applied to Geneva Medical College in Geneva, New York (later Hobart College), the college did not wish to offend her colleague as it received generous donations from Quakers. The dean decided to ask the students at Geneva to vote on whether Blackwell should be admitted, decreeing that only a unanimous vote would get her in. The sons of farmers and tradesman at Geneva voted yes with the accompanying statement: "...one of the radical principles of a Republican Government is the universal education of both sexes...."

Blackwell studied in England and Paris after her graduation, and returned to New York in 1851 to establish a medical practice. This was difficult as she was barred from the city's hospitals and dispensaries, and no one would rent her rooms to use as an office. Blackwell bought a house and began to attract patients by giving lectures on the principles of hygiene. In 1853, Blackwell opened a part-time dispensary for poor women. After several years of fundraising, it became a full-fledged hospital, the New York Infirmary for Women and Children.

Marie Zakrzewska may have been even more important in opening medical careers to women than Elizabeth Blackwell. She emigrated from Germany to the U.S. in 1853, believing that the U.S. offered more opportunities for women physicians. She did become a doctor, with the help of Elizabeth Blackwell and Harriot Hunt, among others. In 1862, she founded the New England Hospital for Women and Children, a new training hospital for women doctors. Zakrzewska always saw separatism as a means to an end—proving that women doctors were competent — and thus paving the way for their admission to the medical community as a whole.

In 1853, **Dr. Clemence Sophia Lozier** graduated at age 40 at the top of her class from the Eclectic Central Medical College in Syracuse, New York. She not only established a large and successful medical practice, she was also an outspoken advocate of women's equality and headed the New York City Suffrage League for many years. In 1863, she founded the New York Medical College and Hospital for Women, the third women's hospital in the country.

Mary Putnam-Jacobi was one of the outstanding female medical activists during this period. She received her medical degree in 1864, and was the first woman to be elected to the distinguished roster of the New York Academy of Medicine (1880). Putnam-Jacobi was an outspoken critic of inequities in the medical profession and did not hesitate to express her feminist views through correspondence with colleagues, and in pamphlets and articles that she wrote. One of her pamphlets, published in 1894, "Common Sense Applied to Woman Suffrage," outlined some of the profound changes taking place as women's participation in modern industrial life increased. She pointed out that working women were no longer dependent on men's financial support, thus removing the basis for men having the right to control their wife's earnings and property.[47]

Key Women Lawyers

> No woman shall degrade herself by practicing law in New York especially if I can save her.... 'Women's Rights Women' are uncommonly loud and offensive of late. I loathe the lot.
>
> —George Templeton Strong, Columbia University Trustee[48]

Frances Willard, a renowned temperance leader, was one of the first individuals to recognize the importance of legal skills in furthering the goals of the temperance movement. In 1873 she suggested that a committee on law should be appointed "to address the Union from time to time until all are thoroughly familiar with the temperance law of their state." She further advised her state captains to provide legal assistance to wives who had the courage to appear in court against the men destroying their homes. Willard also requested that petitions, appeals to voters, and other legal documents should be prepared by the law committee.

Ada Kepley, credited with being the first woman law graduate in the U.S., was active in both the suffrage and the temperance movements. Kepley gained a great deal of notoriety when she began to print the names of local men who frequented a saloon across from her apartment in a newspaper she published. Interest in her paper was as avid as in today's tabloids. The paper was eagerly devoured by her temperance colleagues, as well as the simply curious. Kepley's reporting apparently resulted in a number of family fights, and church and neighborhood quarrels. Once a saloonkeeper's son tried to shoot her, but she continued her "tavern scene" reporting for a number of years.

Temperance activists were often ridiculed as hatchet-wielding, eccentric old maids who lacked conjugal satisfaction. Then, as now, these negative stereotypes were promulgated to sabotage women's efforts. **J. Ellen Foster**, a prominent temperance and suffrage activist, decimated the stereotypes. She was young, married, and often laughingly related to temperance audiences that she read Blackstone, an eighteenth-century English jurist, while rocking her babies. She gained prominence as the first woman to litigate before the Iowa Supreme Court. She later gained national prominence as a temperance speaker, traveling throughout the U.S. to talk about prohibition.

Nebraska's first woman lawyer, **Ada Bittenbinder** was similarly involved in suffrage and temperance work after her admission to the bar in 1882. She served as superintendent of temperance legislation for the national organization in 1888, and repeatedly appeared before congressional committees to advocate bills proposed by her organization. Bittenbinder was unsuccessful when she attempted to prohibit the sale of liquor in the nation's capital and federal territories. She was responsible for writing the National Prohibitory Amendment Guide in 1889, that provided guidelines for organizing and managing temperance petition campaigns. She later ran for Supreme Court judge on the Prohibition Party ticket but was defeated.

Alice Minick, another Nebraska woman lawyer active in both the suffrage and temperance movements, came from a tradition of social reformers. Her father, a staunch abolitionist, made her home a station on the Underground Railroad during her childhood. After Alice was widowed in 1888 at age 43, she entered the University of Nebraska Law School, and graduated three years later "with fine grades." She was, however, unable to find but a few clients after she had set up her practice. Minick reported in her memoirs that her encounters with trial lawyers and judges had not been encouraging, having noted a "chilly atmosphere" whenever she entered a courtroom. After years of seeking redress in the courts for families devastated by alcohol, she became a strong advocate of prohibition by addressing the many social ills associated with intemperance.

Ellen Martin became dedicated to the suffrage movement after being admitted to the bar in 1876. She is believed to have formed the first female law partnership in the nation with another female attorney, Mary Frederick Perry. Both women spent much of their careers campaigning for suffrage and women's rights. Martin's shrewd interpretation of the Lombard, Illinois, city charter that women were legally entitled to vote in municipal elections earned her national attention. After winning her argument, she was able to organize and lead a delegation of women to demand the vote. Her achievement was considered a major victory by her suffragette colleagues in other cities.

Mary Lease, considered one of the greatest orators of her time, commanded the attention of audiences of up to 20,000 people. In response, she was frequently taunted in the newspapers for her fiery oratory. Reporters delighted in referring to her by such names as the "Iron-jawed Woman of Kansas," "Red Dragon," and the "She-lawyer." She was the oldest child of an Irish political activist who died in prison during the Civil War. As a child, Lease had no choice but to work to help support her family, and by age 15 had earned her teaching certificate. She later married a pharmacist who was unable to support their family. Lease had to become the family breadwinner yet again. To do so, she took in laundry, earning a mere 50 cents a day.

After learning that she was reading while doing the laundry, a local lawyer suggested that she might as well be reading and studying law. She followed his advice, and it took her less than a year to prepare for the Kansas bar examination as at that time, no college or law school was required for lawyers to practice in Kansas. After passing the bar, she let it be known that she never intended to charge fees for her services because lawyers had a special duty to help the poor and work for social justice. Eventually she became active in Kansas politics, drawing the wrath of a prominent Kansas senator, John Ingalls. He believed that women had no place in politics, saying, "Mrs. Lease would be better off mending her children's stockings." Lease was undaunted by his remarks, and eventually had the final word. She campaigned against Ingalls, and through her dogged determination was successful in ending his 16-year career in the Senate.

Lease moved to New York City in 1900 to work as a political reporter for Joseph Pulitzer's liberal *New York World*. She continued to be a popular speaker on social issues such as suffrage, birth control, and labor organizing. She opened a law office on the Lower East Side of Manhattan to provide free legal services to the poor. She paid the rent out of her own pocket, and refused to accept a cent from her clients. Later, Lease was proud to boast that she never lost a case that went before a jury, and never charged a client a fee. Unfortunately, she was totally destitute.

Detroit's **Martha Strickland** followed the same creed of assisting poor women for free. She wrote extensively on the status of women in the law, urging female attorneys to work vigorously on behalf of equality for women. Montana's first woman lawyer, Ella Haskell, was admitted to the bar in 1889. She also took charity cases and became active in state politics. Her primary interest was in causing social change in areas affecting women and children.

As the above examples demonstrate, women lawyers were often benevolent in a profession that had a reputation for striving for wealth and power. For this, they received ridicule. **Catherine McCulloch** and **Sophonisa Breckenridge** were warned by male colleagues that their work on behalf of women's causes and the poor, was jeopardizing their careers. A senior member of the Evanston bar also told McCulloch that if she wanted to be successful in her profession, she would have to stop spending so much time on church, temperance, and suffrage causes. He argued that the very people who asked her to speak for free for the love of the cause brought all their paying legal business to male lawyers. McCulloch later wrote that she had to admit that he was right. Notwithstanding, she was unwilling to give up her commitment to social and legislative reform, nor was she willing to discontinue providing legal assistance to the poor.

Crystal Eastman dared to tackle taboo issues such as unsafe conditions in the work place, representing the new face of women lawyers in the early 1900s, who began to address increasingly complex social issues. After graduating from Vassar with honors, she earned her law degree in 1907. She later was appointed to the New York State Employer's Liability Commission, and was responsible for drafting the New York State Workmen's Compensation Law. Her book *Work Accidents and the Law* is believed to have been the definitive work responsible for major reform of factory conditions throughout the United States. Eastman was equally committed to the causes of suffrage, birth-control, labor reform, and world peace. She also helped to found the American Civil Liberties Union to defend conscientious objectors during World War I.[49]

Chapter Three
Women Attempt to Reform Society

Introduction

The women's suffrage movement was only one of many reform movements in the nineteenth century. The idea of becoming "moral agents" to make the world a better place appealed to middle- and upper- class women, who tended to have both time and energy, as well as limited access to the public sphere. Hundreds, and eventually thousands, of women turned their attention to eradicating social evil from American society. Women were greatly involved in the movements to eliminate slavery, pass prohibition laws, improve women's education, and to reform the callous, and often brutal, treatment of the sick, the indigent, the criminals and the insane.[1]

Although the impetus behind these reform movements was not to improve the lives of women specifically, their crusading work served as a training ground, and the organizations that sprang up allowed women to achieve greater participation in social action. Many of the activists in these movements spent all their time putting themselves on the line. They traveled around the country, marched, preached, taught, set up countless meetings under less than ideal conditions, and published endless documents trying to gain public attention and support for their causes. Although men generally held the leadership roles in many of the reform organizations, the worker bees were often women.[2]

Unfortunately, many of these reform movements lacked effective weapons to fight for the demands of women. The only tactics they had at their disposal were speeches, petitions, and the resolutions their organizations had adopted. The frequency of meetings to share ideas and motivate reformers led to the charge that the "women did nothing but talk," insinuating that the "talking" and "flurry of activities" going on at these conventions was more important to the women than meaningful accomplishments.[3]

Through these other reform movements, activists learned how to organize and effectively communicate to a wide audience. Their confidence in their ability to influence broad social change led to lobbying for a variety of women's issues. Their dedicated efforts resulted in a number of reforms, including expanded education and professional opportunities, fairer divorce and child custody laws, the right to retain control of their earnings and property, and, eventually, the right to vote.[4]

Working Toward Suffrage

> The right of any citizens of the United States to vote shall not be denied or abridged by the United States or by any State on account of sex.
> —Nineteenth Amendment,
> U.S. Constitution
> (Ratified August 18, 1920)[5]

The fight for the right of women to vote can be summed up in two words: horrendously difficult. The history of this prolonged struggle is fraught with drama, political intrigue, dissension among leaders, and opposition from a number of quarters. It took more than 70 years from the first women's rights convention in Seneca Falls in 1848 to the final ratification of the Nineteenth Amendment in 1920. And over 50 years elapsed between the first successful suffrage referendum in Kansas in 1867 and the Nineteenth Amendment's passage in 1920.

The cost in human terms for women to achieve the vote over such a prolonged period is immeasurable. It is best summed up by a "first-hand account" from Carrie Chapman Catt and Nettie Rogers Shuler, two women on the scene of the final struggle:

> Hundreds of women gave the accumulated possibilities of an entire lifetime, thousands gave years of their lives, hundreds of thousands gave constant interest and such aid as they could. It was a continuous, seemingly endless, chain of activity. Young suffragists who helped forge the last links of that chain were not born when it began. Old suffragists who forged the first links were dead when it ended.... It is doubtful if any man, even among suffrage men, ever realized what the suffrage struggle came to mean to women before the end was allowed in America.... Not all women in all the States of the Union were in the struggle. There were some women in every state who knew nothing about it. But most women in all the States were at least on the periphery of its effort and interest when they were not in the heart of it. To them all its success became a monumental thing.[6]

The suffrage movement gained momentum after the Seneca Falls Convention in 1848, but nothing that could be considered to be of national importance. In the 1870s, the movement was still small and divided. By the end of the 1880s, however, it was gaining more support. In part, this was because the suffragettes were learning to work the system more and using a variety of political strategies to push reform. They organized state suffrage associations, began publicity campaigns for educating the public, petitioned states for suffrage referenda, and constantly bombarded Congress for an amendment to the Constitution. Their persistence and energy did not, however, lead to immediate success.

American women were the largest disfranchised group of people in U.S. history, and retained this position longer than any other group.[7]

Obstacles to Suffrage

It is not enough to describe the opposition to female suffrage as based on pervasive sexist attitudes about women's role in society. By the second decade of the twentieth century, some of the taboos and restrictions applying to women had been swept away. True, some of the opposition was based on prejudices against women, but this does not explain the multitude of organized fights that occurred with such intensity during the beginning of the new century. It took many years for the leaders of the suffrage movement to comprehend the amount of overt hostility so many different sources directed against them. Opposition to a woman's right to vote came predominantly from a few groups: the South, high society women, brewery and liquor interests, and big business. Unfortunately, women activists and the suffrage groups themselves often did not agree on initiatives, so infighting became another obstacle.[8]

Southern Opposition

Male leaders in Southern states aggressively opposed the right of women to vote. Historians have largely attributed this reaction to intense opposition to the right of African Americans (men and women) to vote. Many Southern leaders feared the possibility of "women reformers" demanding the end of Jim Crow laws, including the poll tax, which had disenfranchised the male Negro population in defiance of the Fourteenth and Fifteenth Amendments.[9] In addition, there was significant fear that the second section of the Fourteenth Amendment might be enforced if women had the vote. This section punished states that denied male citizens the right to vote (only criminals and rebels could be denied suffrage). Southern states thus lobbied for states' rights and opposed a federal mandate regarding women's suffrage.[10]

In addition, there was a lack of support among Southern women. These women had lived under the oppressive climate of slavery—

whether they approved of its practice or not—for a long time. Southern society as a whole had become very repressive insofar as the "peculiar institution" was concerned and exceedingly conformist with regard to any type of reform activity. The institution of slavery itself tended to stifle any tendency individuals might have toward reform or dissent.[11]

White Southern women were in a form of human bondage themselves, cloaked under the guise of the often glamorized "Southern chivalry" that held them in their place. Many were conscious that this highly praised lifestyle served only to keep them firmly entrenched within the domestic sphere, yet they were both entrapped and isolated. Their condition limited the possibility for reform to develop in the South as it had in other parts of the country where women had not been quite so restrained. Any Southern woman who did not fully embrace the Southern plantation life had no choice but to leave or face social ostracism.[12] Unfortunately, once slavery ended, many middle- and upper-class Southern women supported a platform that served only to extend racial discrimination.

A Southern women's suffrage conference agreed with their Southern male representatives that suffrage should be settled on a state-by-state basis. The Southern women were convinced that suffrage achieved via individual states would prove a double blessing: it would enfranchise them and insure white supremacy by doubling the white electorate. They were confident that even if African-American women were enfranchised, it would be as easy to deprive them of this right as it had been to deprive African-American men (perhaps, even easier).[13]

Why Southerners were so concerned about African-American women getting the vote is unclear. As history shows, they had no difficulty keeping African-American men away from the polls in spite of the Fifteenth Amendment that specifically gave African Americans and former slaves the right to vote (see Chapter 2), and at one time, repeal of the Fifteenth Amendment loomed as a distinct possibility. Recent social historians have attempted to place a more positive light on the racist actions of white suffragists, pointing out they had no other choice but to exclude African Americans if suffrage were to have a chance of winning.

Nonetheless, by taking this stance, white women were following the same path as male abolitionists had taken against them—denying the rights of one group to ensure the rights of another. But most white women, not just in the South, shared the predominant and rarely challenged racist views of the times.[14]

Suffragist leaders were caught in a dilemma during the North versus South controversy. It might have been difficult for such well-known leaders as Elizabeth Cady Stanton and Susan B. Anthony to ignore their past record of supporting freedom for African Americans, but their bitterness toward giving the vote to foreign-born immigrants (who were often unschooled, and unable to read or write English) opened the door to bigotry. It was only a short step from requiring education as the basis for enfranchisement to supporting the Southerner's claims of "white supremacy," particularly such Southern demands as granting suffrage only to women who could read and write and pay taxes.[15]

In March 1919, Walter White, a young author and investigator, assessed the charged situation after women's suffrage had been defeated in the United States Senate—by a single vote. This defeat was possible, he said, only because of an alliance between Southern senators and a conservative contingency from the West and Northeast who had their own political agendas. White wrote in a letter to suffragette Mary Church Terrell: "If they could get the suffrage amendment without enfranchising colored women, they would do it in a moment; all of them are mortally afraid of the South."[16] Then as now, political alliances were necessary to pass legislation in Congress, and the Southern states had much more power than they do today because of their significant populations; many Western states had only recently been admitted to the union and had low populations.

High Society Women's Opposition

Female opposition to women's suffrage came from outside the South as well. Almost without exception, the women who formed well-organized anti-suffrage groups were well-to-do women of irreproachable social standing, including wives of government officials and industry leaders. The members of these organizations appeared at legislative hearings, sent telegrams, distributed literature and sought the assistance of "male counsel," as well as newspapers sympathetic to their cause. They became known as "remonstrants."[17]

One of the arguments the opposition used was that suffrage would add a burden to women's more important domestic responsibilities. There was no need for political suffrage for married women; their husbands would adequately represent them and look out for their best interests. These arguments were designed to appeal to well-to-do women, whose housework was performed by servants, and who felt they had nothing to gain by the vote. These campaigns by high-society women were not deemed threatening by the suffragettes, who believed that these "remonstrants" were actually serving as fronts for other anti-suffrage groups, particularly the liquor interests, a very potent force opposing suffrage.[18]

It was not until the early 1900s, however, that the suffrage leaders adopted the "society plan" wherein they undertook efforts to recruit large numbers of socially prominent and politically influential women into the fold. Their efforts also included convincing middle- and upper-class women who were involved in the women's clubs that suffrage would be of benefit to their efforts to improve their communities. The growing numbers of college-educated women, many of them professionals, were also targeted for membership.[19]

Brewery and Liquor Interests' Opposition

The women suffrage leaders were politically savvy enough to recognize the "rich ladies" anti-suffrage movement for what it was—a minor annoyance. The brewery and liquor interests were formidable enemies that could not be written off easily. The women leaders understood the motivation behind the alcoholic beverage industry opposition to suffrage. The alcohol industry was afraid that if women could vote, prohibition would soon follow. [20]

The brewery and liquor interests were determined to use any means possible to stifle interference with their profits, and women's suffrage was seen as a threat to their business. They used their considerable financial resources and influence, to develop a highly powerful political backing, but were careful to operate in the background. Their anonymity was shattered when a Senate investigating committee disclosed their clandestine anti-suffrage activities in several defeats of state referenda that would have granted women suffrage.[21]

Big Business and Other Forces' Opposition

There were many other anti-suffrage forces at work that were less well-organized than the brewery and liquor industry. The political machines usually came out against suffrage, although this activity diminished after Tammany Hall, the powerful Democratic machine in New York City, gave up in 1917. Politicians appeared to oppose women as voters due to their lack of susceptibility to bribery and their strong inclinations for reforms that ranged from abolition of child labor to better sewage control to decorrupting politics.[22] Churches of many faiths were initially opposed to female suffrage, although, eventually, the clergy split on the issue.

Big business was another facet of the problem, but it was difficult to link these forces to an organized effort. There was no visible nationwide mobilization, but evidence of involvement by railroad, oil, and manufacturing interests was unmistakable whenever suffrage came up for legislative or referendum action. During a congressional investigation, it was revealed that the meat packing company Swift & Company was shown to have made secret contributions to anti-suffrage groups. An appeal to Nebraska voters against women's suffrage in 1914 carried the signatures of railroad and municipal transit executives, bankers, other businessmen, and ministers. And two directors of the national women's anti-suffrage organization were wives of directors of railroads.[23]

It is not difficult to understand why big business interests were opposed to women getting the vote. Populist legislation was being enacted fairly rapidly in the early 1900s, much of which appeared to threaten the vested interests of business. The Federal Income Tax was authorized by the Sixteenth Amendment to the Constitution in 1913. Popular election of U.S. Senators was provided through the Seventeenth Amendment, also enacted in 1913. The Federal Reserve banking system had been instituted as well as the Tariff Commission, the Federal Trade Commission, and new anti-trust legislation. Further, business leaders believed that if women were to get the vote, they would vote to improve the conditions of working women (including equity in pay scales) and to outlaw child labor.[24]

Dissension Among Women Activists

Women activists and the suffragettes themselves bear some of the blame for the delay in winning the right to vote. They were never in accord, from the beginning, on what was worth a fight. Some factions were concerned with other legal rights and did not feel the vote was necessary. Others felt that education should be insisted upon as a woman's basic right so that she could become a better wife and mother, and yet another group insisted that only voting rights were imperative. Each of these reforms was important in its own way. However, the resulting controversies and divisiveness interfered with progress.

An early rift in the forces working to get women the right to vote occurred during the debate on the Fourteenth Amendment, which was ratified in 1868. The main argument related to greater rights for African Americans and women, and where the emphasis should be placed, if there had to be a choice between the two. Then, when the Fifteenth Amendment passed without adding the word "sex," the rift deepened. The first federal women's suffrage amendment was introduced to the House of Representatives in 1868. In 1878, when Senator A.A. Sargent of California introduced a female suffrage measure, it became known as the "Anthony Amendment" which, without any change in wording, was used until finally passed by Congress as the Nineteenth Amendment in 1920.[25]

The actual split in the women's movement occurred in May 1869. A convention of woman's rights activists had been convened in January to discuss women's suffrage under the auspices of the American Equal Rights Association. This organization was comprised of women and men. Susan B. Anthony and Elizabeth Cady Stanton, acting on the belief that only women could be standard bearers for women's suffrage effectively mutinied and formed the National Woman Suffrage Association (the National). In November 1869, a second organization was set up, called the American Woman Suffrage Association (the American). Lucy Stone was associated with the American. To keep out the so-called undesirables, this association was organized on a delegate basis. Membership in the American was open only to members of "recognized" suffrage organizations. These two groups operated independently for over 20 years due to basic philosophical differences over the appropriate methods for getting women the vote.[26]

The National Woman Suffrage Association, reflecting the philosophies of its founders Elizabeth Cady Stanton and Susan B. Anthony, sought to work with anyone who supported the suffrage movement—regardless of their views on other matters. Consequently, in its earlier years, the National was recognized as being both aggressive and unorthodox, even referred to as "radical." The National was against any candidate, regardless of political party affiliation, who ignored the suffrage question. And the National was willing to take up the battle for distressed women, including underpaid seamstresses whatever their circumstances—even "fallen" or divorced women. The National promoted a wide variety of feminist reforms in its short-lived publication, *Revolution*.[27]

The American Woman Suffrage Association differed markedly. The American was highly selective of the causes it was willing to embrace and could be categorized as "conservative." Lucy Stone, one of the founders, did not want the suffrage cause tarnished by concern with other issues such as labor conditions for working women and the associated trade unions, divorce, or the social evil of intemperance. Julia Ward Howe, an honored lay preacher, and the author of "The Battle Hymn of the

Republic," personified the aura of prestige and propriety that the American organization desired both to be and to portray. The American developed grassroots support for women's suffrage through state-level organizations. Through its publication, *The Woman's Journal*, the organization tried to make suffrage for women and feminist reforms seem less radical and more consistent with widely-shared American values.[28]

However, by 1887, merger negotiations had begun between the two suffrage organizations and were consummated at a joint convention in February 1890. Alice Stone Blackwell, the gifted daughter of Lucy Stone and Henry Blackwell, was key in facilitating the unification. The resulting nationwide suffrage organization, with Elizabeth Cady Stanton as its president, was called The National American Woman Suffrage Association (NAWSA). Such a merger was possible because of factors that developed during the last 20 years of the nineteenth century.[29]

For one, a profound change of public attitude had occurred. Female suffrage, although maybe not yet generally accepted, was no longer on the fringes. The annual convention of the National had become a social event in Washington, D.C., complete with White House teas and receptions. Younger leaders were rising within the organizations—women who had not experienced the economic hardships that the pioneers, such as Lucy Stone and Susan B. Anthony, had experienced. The younger leaders within the suffrage movement didn't need the same courage and conviction that had been necessary for those pioneers to survive. The younger leaders were also more likely to be professionals, writers, and women of substantial means, as opposed to the earlier leaders who had been primarily housewives or single women.[30]

State Efforts Toward Suffrage

Some of the activists within the women's suffrage movement advocated state-by-state efforts as opposed to federal action. However, gaining suffrage through amendment of state constitutions was a long and arduous process. From 1870 to 1910, there were 480 campaigns in 33 states, working simply to have the issue submitted to the voters. Only 17 of these resulted in actual referendum votes, and only two referenda were successful—Colorado and Idaho. Victory in these two sparsely populated states had little significance in terms of winning suffrage for women nationally. However, the 1893 Colorado referendum was important in that male voters actually went to the polls and gave women the right to vote. When two new states were admitted to the Union—Wyoming in 1890 and Utah in 1896—the number of states granting women the right to vote rose to four.[31]

Conditions relating to referenda varied from state to state, but demonstrated the general obstacles to women's suffrage and particularly the arduousness of a state-by-state approach. In 1890, in South Dakota, for instance, the blazing hot summer and freezing cold fall conditions, combined with the great distances activists had to travel, caused most of the suffrage workers to become ill. And the measure lost by a margin of almost two to one.

In 1887, women in Kansas had won "partial suffrage" and so were able to vote in school or municipal elections. By 1894, these suffragettes had aligned with the political parties. For the 1894 Kansas referendum on suffrage, those women who had aligned with the Republican party found themselves supporting a party platform that opposed suffrage, and thereby, doomed the referendum to failure.

Massachusetts held a mock referendum in 1895 that was so resoundingly defeated that it was thought to set back the women's suffrage effort in the state for more than a decade. The California referendum in 1896 was defeated at the hands of liquor interests who managed to carry the larger counties and thus ensure defeat statewide.[32]

During the 1896 California referendum, wealthy women gave substantial sums of money to the suffrage movement for the first time. Although Jane Stanford (wife of Leland Stanford, and co-grantor of the endowment and establishment of Stanford University) and Millicent Hearst (wife of William Randolph Hearst) made large contributions, the bulk of the funds continued to come from poor seamstresses, washerwomen and the like. A vivid account of the sacrifices these women were willing to make is reported in the writings of Ida Husted Harper, California state chairman of the suffrage publicity committee:[33]

> ...Often, when there was not enough money at headquarters to buy a postage stamp, there would come a timid knock at the door and a poor-dressed woman would enter with a quarter or half dollar, saying, 'I have done without tea this week to bring you this money.' Or a poor little clerk would say, 'I made a piece of fancy work evenings and sold it for this dollar.' Many a woman who worked hard ten hours a day to earn her bread, would come to headquarters and carry home a great armload of circulars to fold and address. And there were teachers and stenographers and other working women who went without a winter coat to give money to this movement for freedom.[34]

Women's Rights in the Early 1900s

As the fight for women's suffrage wore on, its original proponents grew older. At the beginning of the new century, American women were living very different lives than those led by previous generations as the country moved toward industrialization and urbanization. Changes had occurred in the legal position of women—although there were differences in degree from one state to another. The states west of the Alleghenies had never shown legal discrimination against women in its worst forms. Equality before the law, although not in political status, was made part of some Western state constitutions even as they were admitted to the Federal union. In Western states, progress was more rapid than in the East, probably because of their pioneer conditions.[35]

In most of the Eastern states, it took until the first decade of the twentieth century to ensure a few essential legal rights. By 1900, a married woman in most states had gained the right not only to her own property but also to her earnings. But in 1900, a married woman in Pennsylvania still could not enter a business contract without her husband's approval. Historians contend that Eastern states lagged behind because of their stratified society and the difficulty in overcoming their heritage of religion-based beliefs about women's inferiority.[36]

The Southern states presented yet a worse picture. The Southern states' lack of progress can be blamed partly on the slowness of economic recovery after the Civil War; so much of the war was fought on Southern soil. Before the war, few women had earned their own living except for African Americans and poor whites, who had always had to work to support themselves and their families. Little progress had been made, even during the later decades of the century, to remove existing legal and political restrictions. Conditions about other specifics varied from state to state by 1900. For example, in Louisiana, where the discriminatory provision of the Code Napoléon inherited from the period of French domination was still in force, a married woman did not have legal title even to the clothes she wore. In Georgia, a woman's earnings belonged to her husband. At the same time, however, a woman in Florida could control her own earnings, and in Mississippi, her property rights were fairly well safe-guarded by the law.[37]

Most historians agree that the greatest gender inequities in every state were in the realm of divorce. The law was punitive when it came to women accused of committing adultery, while the man suffered no penalties. Minnesota required that a woman divorced for adultery forfeit real estate that was her own property. Pennsylvania forbade a woman's disposal of her property if she chose to live with her adulterous partner after her divorce. And it was an almost universally accepted practice that a woman was denied custody of her children after divorce.[38]

Gradually, all states began to legislate more humane and equitable treatment of women, but it took a number of years of bitter struggle before this took place.[39]

The focus on women's rights was not at the forefront from 1896 to 1910, the so-called "doldrums" of the women's suffrage movement. During that time, only six state referenda were held—three in Oregon, one each in Washington, South Dakota, and New Hampshire. All were lost. The issue of female enfranchisement had not been debated on the floor of the Senate since 1887, and had never reached the floor of the House. The suffrage bill had not received a favorable committee report in either house since 1893, and no report at all since 1896. However, by 1909, the women's movement was beginning to focus on one concern—the right to vote—and momentum was beginning to return to the cause of suffrage. The credit for turning this disheartening situation around is given to a young woman who had previously gained her experience in the militant wing of the British suffrage movement, Alice Paul, and to Carrie Chapman Catt.[40]

Catt and Paul helped bring about the final victory for the women suffragists—each in her own way and at different times. Carrie Chapman Catt assumed the presidency of the NAWSA in 1900. Her contribution was that she saw the voting issue as a political one that could only be resolved by political action. She was no amateur reformer and used her skills as a professional organizer to pull together all of the divisive units into a cohesive organization. Creating a trained and experienced staff was one of Catt's foremost goals. Once this mission was achieved, the organization was able to measure up to any demands made on it.[41]

Perhaps, it was this inspired leadership that prompted Miriam Leslie, the wealthy publisher of *Leslie's Weekly*, to personally bequeath to Catt the bulk of her $2 million dollar estate. Leslie's bequest contained the wish that her fortune be directed "to the furtherance of the cause of woman suffrage." These funds marked a magnificent amount for an organization that had heretofore always been in financial crisis.[42]

Paul was a flamboyant militant and organizer, who had the charisma to garner tremendous numbers of supporters around her, reaching the peak of her popularity between 1913 and 1916. After being appointed chair of the congressional committee for the national suffrage amendment in 1912, she organized a parade of women, the day before Woodrow Wilson's inauguration in 1913. The police's lack of action in protecting the women from the antagonistic spectators angered the public and gave much-needed momentum back to the suffrage movement.

The number of women in the work force had reached over 7 million by 1910, up from 4 million in 1890, while the U.S. population had increased from almost 63 million to over 92 million.[43] Most of the women in the work force were in domestic occupations, but some women had taken government jobs, and the typewriter's invention in 1867 had provided an impetus for more job opportunities. Women's work in sweatshops and textile factories no longer required protection, as some labor laws had been established. However, most of the women who were working were not earning salaries on a par with men, and many in industry worked in poor conditions without the benefit of any union organization. Women's work could no longer be considered something done solely in personal service of father or husband, thus there was no longer any basis for a man controlling a woman's property and earnings. And, with this new level of independence, there was no reason why a man should represent a woman politically.[44] Against this backdrop, women were making significant inroads into education, especially higher education and were starting to join the ranks of professionals in such fields as medicine and law.

There were other forces at work besides the suffragist movement that finally turned the tide of victory: World War I. This war—like the Civil War—brought an enormous number of women out of the home into new spheres of action. Their avid participation in industrial and public service work profoundly affected their community standing: if democracy began at home, surely the women who were shouldering every aspect of social responsibility while the men were at war were deserving of full political responsibility.[45]

The list of occupations in which women substituted for men during the first world war is impressive. They held jobs in blast furnaces and in the manufacture of steel plate, high explosives, armaments, machine tools, agricultural implements, electrical apparatuses, machine tools, railway, automobile and airplane parts. They also worked in brass and copper smelting and oil refining, and worked in the production of chemicals, fertilizers and leather goods. Thousands of additional women poured into the textile mills, and a host of other nontraditional workplaces.[46]

This wholesale employment of women in occupations in which few or none had worked before raised a new set of questions concerning women's rights that would be debated throughout the century: Should women be allowed to work unlimited hours, and should they be allowed to work only in protected environments?[47]

The NAWSA, with Catt at its head, was very prominent in the war effort and even maintained and financed an overseas hospital in France. The busy suffragists throughout the nation managed to raise and can food, knit, and work for the Red Cross. But Catt wanted to ensure they would never miss a beat in doing what she referred to as "their number one war job"—working for the suffrage cause. Accordingly, the women even took time out from their intense participation in the war effort to stage a last great suffrage parade in New York on October 27, 1917.[48]

This parade was smaller by far than many of the others that had preceded it, particularly the one conducted in 1915, but it was even more effective because of its timing. The women who marched represented every walk of life—farmers, industry workers, doctors, and Red Cross nurses from overseas. Women were obviously supporting the war effort in every city and at every crossroads—how could they continue to be denied the rights of citizenship? The 2,500 women who marched down Fifth Avenue carried placards plastered with signatures of more than a million women.[49]

Although in the first months of 1917 the organization's increasing organized activities in the states were beginning to produce results, this was not enough. The special war session of Congress, which ran from April until October 1917, had been barred from considering anything but war measures. This provided a convenient excuse to delay the suffrage issue for as long as possible. This limitation was removed when Congress reconvened on December 3, 1917. A vote on the Anthony amendment was scheduled in the House for January 10, 1918.[50]

President Wilson made his long-awaited announcement on January 9, 1918, the day before the vote, saying that he had committed himself to supporting the measure. When he had been governor of New Jersey, Wilson had been considered anti-suffrage. Although he had eventually become pro-suffrage, he had not seen his support of the amendment as pivotal to women's suffrage. However, the NAWSA did, if they were to have any chance to pass it through Congress and be ratified by the states.

Wilson may also have changed his stance in order to preserve America's image as a leader in the effort to achieve worldwide democracy. In Great Britain, the House of Commons had passed a female suffrage bill on November 10, 1917. And on the same day that the suffrage amendment passed the American House of Representatives, the resistance of the conservative British House of Lords gave way to approve the bill. During this period, women also had won the vote in most of the provinces of the Dominion of Canada.[51]

The vote on the Anthony amendment in the House of Representatives on January 10, 1918, was 274 to 136, exactly the two-thirds majority required to pass a constitutional amendment. However, it still needed to pass the Senate.[52]

Historians note that the amendment would never have passed without the devotion and support of the men who actively lobbied for its passage. Three of these champions who were counted as determining votes came from sick-beds: Thetus Sims of Tennessee with a broken arm and shoulder, Republican House minority leader James Mann of Illinois who left his hospital bed and was barely able to stand upright, and Henry Barnhart of Indiana, who was carried in on a stretcher during the very last roll call. Representative Frederick Hicks of New York kept faith with his wife, an ardent suffragist who had just died. He left her death-bed to come to Washington for the roll call to ensure that he cast a vote.[53]

These men's dedication worked a miracle: The bulk of the nay votes came from a majority of the Southern states and from the largely industrial states of Massachusetts, Pennsylvania, New Jersey, and Ohio. The vote cut sharply across party lines. The Democrats divided almost evenly—104 in favor to 102 against. Political observers said that the Republicans had their eye on the coming 1920 elections, which accounted for their preponderance of favorable votes. Regardless of the reasons, 165 of the party's faithful voted for the amendment, with only 33 against.[54]

But this was only the House of Representatives. Article V of the Constitution requires approval by both the House and the Senate prior to sending the amendment out to ratification by the states. It took all of 1918 and half of 1919, and the election of a new Congress, to get the suffrage amendment passed by the Senate (on June 4, 1919). Ratification took an additional 14 months—requiring a state-by-state battle. Tennessee was the final and 36th state and here the amendment was ratified by only one vote. The deciding vote was cast by Harry Burn, the youngest member of the legislature, who voted yes after receiving a telegram from his mother urging him to do the right thing and vote in favor of the amendment. Dr. Anna Shaw, President of the NAWSA, from 1904-1915 was terminally ill when the amendment passed the Senate, but she lived long enough to see that the ratification campaign was going well.[55]

The Nineteenth Amendment to the U.S. Constitution was signed by Secretary of State Bainbridge Colby on August 26, 1920, thereby, enfranchising 26 million women of voting age, but the fight was not yet completely over. The last challenge to women's suffrage was not overcome until February 1922, when the U.S. Supreme Court handed down the second of two decisions upholding the Nineteenth Amendment.[56]

KEY WOMEN OF THIS PERIOD

Lucretia Mott (1793-1880)

> Her right to elective franchise, however, is the same, and should be yielded to her, whether she exercises that right or not. Would that men, too, would have no participation in a government recognizing the life-taking principle—retaliation and the sword.... I can see no good reason why women should not participate in such an assemblage, taking part equally with man.

Lucretia Mott's biographers report that she was widely loved and admired by other activists during a period of stormy conflicts and clashing personalities. She had a gentle and non-assuming temperament that endeared her to others. This probably was the characteristic that impressed the young Elizabeth Cady Stanton when they first met in the gallery at the World Anti-Slavery Convention in London in 1840. By the time of the convention, Mott already was a recognized public figure and had gained prominence as a skillful organizer. She had been the founder of the first Female Anti-Slavery Society, and remained ever active, continually trying to bring recruits into the fold. At first, she was somewhat conservative and not wholly supportive of women's franchise, but this was all to change. It was through her alliance with Stanton that the dream of the first women's rights convention—Seneca Falls—became a reality.

The daughter of a sea captain, Lucretia Coffin was born in 1793 on the Island of Nantucket, and was steeped in the tradition of female equality that grew out of mens' long absences at sea. Seaside women had no choice but to be independent. The young Lucretia became a teacher while still in her teens and deeply resented that women were paid much less than men for doing the same work. When she married James Mott, the couple settled in Philadelphia, where she taught briefly in a Quaker School. She was ordained a minister at the age of 28, and when the Quakers split on matters of doctrine, she and her husband joined the more liberal wing. Subsequently, the Motts became active abolitionists and their home became a busy way station on the Underground Railroad.

Mott delivered the opening and closing address at the Seneca Falls Convention, and her husband James chaired the proceedings at the Wesleyan Chapel. The Declaration of Sentiments was issued as a result of the 1848 Seneca Falls Convention. Another outgrowth of the convention was Mott's book, *Discourse on Women* (1850), in which she discussed the disabilities of women.

Mott was elected the president of the American Equal Rights Association at its organizing meeting in 1866. And in 1867, she joined others in the founding of the Free Religious Association. She was active in the causes of women's rights, peace, and liberal religion until her death. Mott died in 1880, having spent her last few years trying to reconcile the differences between the two main suffragist organizations—the National and the American.[57]

Sojourner Truth (c. 1797 – 1883)

> I could work as much and eat as much as a man, when I could get it, and bear the lash as well as a man. And ain't I a woman?

Sojourner Truth was born a slave in Ulster County, New York, and was named Isabella by her owner. He was a cruel man and flogged her in the presence of the man she wished to marry, thereby further humiliating her. When she finally married a man whom her owner approved, she bore 13 children—most of whom were sold into slavery. After New York State freed its slaves in 1827, Isabella found refuge with a Quaker family and adopted the name Isabella Van Wagener. When she set out on her own as a traveling preacher in 1843, she adopted a new name—Sojourner Truth.

Her religious fervor led her to associate with reformers and she became an active leader in the abolitionist movement. In 1850, she took up the women's rights movement after she attended a Worcester, Massachusetts, convention.

She already had gained prominence as a passionate speaker, and shared the podium with renowned abolitionist Frederick Douglass, when she attended a women's rights convention in Akron, Ohio, in 1851. Fearful that she might harm the suffrage cause with a plea for abolition instead, some of the delegates pleaded with the chairperson, Frances Dana Gage, not to give her the floor, but Gage ignored their pleas. Truth remained unruffled throughout the jeering she received from the audience, and when she did take the platform upon Gage's insistence, her dignity and presence were awe-inspiring.

She turned the full force of her eloquence on the previous speaker, a male minister who had been ridiculing the weakness and helplessness of women, sufficient reasons in his mind for not entrusting women with the vote. She joined the indignation of her race to the indignation of her sex, in a manner that few women there had ever heard before. The room hushed, and everyone began to listen intently to her few simple words: "That man over there says that woman needs to be helped into carriages and lifted over ditches.... Nobody ever helps me into carriages, or over mud-puddles or gives me any best place. And ain't I a woman? I could work as much and eat as much as a man, when I could get it, and bear the lash as well as a man. And ain't I a woman?"

She drove home the similarity between her life and that of the women in the audience by concluding, "If my cup won't hold but a pint, and yours holds a quart, wouldn't ye be mean not to let me have my little half measure full?" Truth left the platform amid roars of applause. Gage later wrote that she had never seen anything in her life to equal the magical influence that subdued "the snobbish spirit of the day and turned the sneers and jeers of the crowd into notes of respect and admiration."

In October 1864, President Abraham Lincoln received her in the White House. After the Civil War, Truth continued to travel and lecture on women's rights.[58]

Elizabeth Cady Stanton (1815 - 1902)

> I should feel exceedingly diffident to appear before you at this time, having never before spoken in public, were I not nerved by a sense of right and duty, did I not feel that the time had come for the question of woman's wrongs to be laid before the public, did I not believe that woman herself must do this work; for woman alone can understand the height, the depth, the length and the breadth of her degradation.

Women Attempt to Reform Society

The daughter of a judge, Elizabeth Cady of Johnstown, New York, received the finest education: the Johnstown Academy and Emma Willard's Troy Female Seminary. She also spent hours in her father's office listening to the people who came to him with their legal problems, many of them wives and daughter of farmers. Judge Cady often helped them out by dipping into his own pocket to help with their expenses; but he said to all of them that they had no legal redress. This made an indelible impact on Elizabeth Cady. She also had an early introduction to the abolitionist movement through her cousin Gerrit Smith and his daughter Elizabeth Smith (Miller), including encounters with fugitive slaves at the Smith's house.

In 1840, she married abolitionist leader Henry Stanton. She insisted that the word "obey" be omitted from the wedding ceremony. On their honeymoon, they went to London to attend the World Anti-Slavery Convention, where she met Lucretia Mott, an official delegate to the Convention. Stanton was incensed by the treatment that the official women delegates to the Convention had received; they were not allowed to be seated because of their sex.

Her own activism, however, was sparked once her family moved to Seneca Falls, New York. She was now a small-town housewife with all of the associated drudgery and isolation. She spoke frequently on the subject of women's rights and circulated petitions that helped secure passage by the New York legislature in March 1848 of a bill granting property rights to married women. When Lucretia Mott visited nearby Waterloo, New York, the women together issued a call for the first women's rights convention. The Seneca Falls Convention, held in the Wesleyan Chapel in July 1848, was where Stanton made the speech quoted above. Stanton wrote the *Declaration of Sentiments* that was adopted at the Seneca Falls Convention and also introduced the resolution for women's suffrage that was finally adopted after much debate.

From 1851, she worked closely with Susan B. Anthony, and they developed a lifelong partnership dedicated to the cause of women's suffrage. Stanton, the better orator and writer, was perfectly complemented by Anthony, the organizer and tactician. Among their earliest targets were the laws that discriminated against married women, denying them the right to hold property, or wages, or guardianship of their children. In 1854, she addressed the New York legislature (it was almost unheard of for women to speak in public, so this was unprecedented). By 1860, that address bore fruit, as New York granted married women the rights to their wages and equal guardianship of their children.

Stanton was the founding genius of the women's rights movement. In May 1869, she helped organize the National Woman Suffrage Association and became founding president; she was to retain that post throughout the organization's 21-year existence. Stanton was the principal author of the *Woman's Declaration of Rights* presented at the Centennial Exposition in Philadelphia in 1876. She took up not only the cause of women's suffrage, but also favored more liberal divorce laws. After her seven children were grown, she toured the country calling for voting rights, coeducation, dress reform, and other advances. The so-called Anthony amendment, first introduced in 1878, was authored by Stanton. When the National Woman Suffrage Association merged with the American Woman Suffrage Association in 1890, she was elected president of the new National American Women Suffrage Association; she held the post until 1892. Her activism did not diminish with her age.[59]

Lucy Stone (1818 – 1893)

> I expect to plead not for the slave only, but for suffering humanity everywhere. Especially do I mean to labor for the elevation of my sex.

Lucy Stone recognized early on what it meant to work as hard as any man and yet be regarded as his inferior. On a small farm in western Massachusetts, Lucy was one of seven children born to a work-worn mother, who could only exclaim when Lucy was born, "I am sorry it is a girl. A woman's life is so hard." Her mother's attitude grew out of her own life on the farm. She had to milk eight cows, for instance, just before giving birth. A sudden thunderstorm had called all hands to the field; saving the hay crop was more important than safeguarding a mother on the verge of labor. The women not only had the household tasks as their responsibility, but a heavy load of dairy work as well. Stone recalled, "There was only one will in our house, and that was my father's."

Early on, Stone began to rebel against the restrictions placed on her because of gender. When she began teaching at age 16 to earn enough money to attend college, she was irritated because her salary was lower than that paid to men. Her determination to attend college derived in part from her desire to better herself and, in part, from her resolve to learn Hebrew and Greek so that she could determine if the passages in the Bible that seemingly had given men the right to dominate women had been properly translated! She also wanted to prepare for a career as a speaker against slavery and in favor of women's rights.

She entered Oberlin College in 1843. She was one of the earliest women to graduate from the regular course offered to men, as distinguished from the "literary" course previously offered to women. Lucy was not a "prized student" among the young ladies who attended Oberlin. She and her classmate Antoinette Brown were regarded as rebels, as they refused to conform to the standards set for "proper young ladies." Despite her rebelliousness, Stone graduated in the top of her class in 1847.

After her graduation, she was hired as an agent by the Anti-Slavery Society. Because they did not wish for her to speak on the subject of women's rights, Stone and the organization compromised; she would speak on women's rights on a professional basis, not when she was representing the Society. This compromise was arranged after she told the organization, "I was a woman before I was abolitionist; I must speak for the women." She gave anti-slavery talks on weekends. She gave women's rights speeches during the week at her own expense or by charging admission.

When she spoke out in favor of abolishing slavery, she had the support of the anti-slavery groups. She had no such support in her one-person campaign to obtain equal rights for women. She later wrote: "When I undertook my solitary battle for woman's rights outside the little circle of abolitionists, I knew nobody who sympathized with my ideas." She was finally joined by others supporting the cause of women's rights when she led in calling a national convention on women's rights in Worcester, Massachusetts, in 1850. During this Convention, her speech converted Susan B. Anthony to the cause.

Her opponents hoped that her marriage to Henry Blackwell in 1855 would put an end to her career, but their hopes were dashed. The marriage made two advocates for women's rights instead of one—and eventually three. Henry Blackwell, brother of Dr. Elizabeth Blackwell, Lucy Stone, and their daughter, Alice Stone Blackwell, covered nearly the entire span of the first wave of the women's rights movement, from 1848 to 1920.

When Lucy Stone married Henry Blackwell, she was one of the first women to refuse to take her husband's last name after marriage. She preferred to be addressed as "Mrs. Stone." And she led to the coining of the term "Lucy Stoner" for a married woman who keeps her original surname. She may also have been one of the first brides to read a set of prepared wedding vows alongside her groom. The prepared vows they read aloud as they held hands were very specific as to the role of the wife and husband in this relationship. The statement declared their lack of obedience to marriage laws that refused to recognize the wife as an "independent, rational being, while they confer upon the husband an injurious and unnatural superiority." They even went so far as to enumerate the various laws of marriage to which they jointly protested:

"We protest especially against the laws which give the husband:

1. The custody of the wife's person.
2. The exclusive control and guardianship of their children.
3. The sole ownership of her personal and use of her real estate, unless previously settled upon her, or placed in the hands of trustees, as in the case of minors, lunatics and idiots.

4. The absolute right to the product of her industry.
5. Also against laws which give to the widower so much larger and more permanent interest in the property of his deceased wife than they give to the widow in that of the deceased husband.
6. Finally, against the whole system by which 'the legal existence of the wife is suspended during marriage' so that, in most States, she neither has a legal part in the choice of her residence, nor can she make a will, nor sue or be sued in her own name, nor inherit property."

Stone retired from public affairs for a time after presiding over the 1856 National Woman's Rights Convention to care for her daughter. In 1866, Stone helped found the American Equal Rights Association. In 1867, she helped organize and was elected president of the New Jersey Woman Suffrage Association.

Stone helped establish the conservative American Woman Suffrage Association in November 1869. She raised money to help launch the weekly *Woman's Journal* in 1870, and in 1872, she and her husband succeeded Mary A. Livermore as editors. After the two associations merged in 1890, she became chairman of the executive board of the merged National American Woman Suffrage Association. Her last lectures were delivered in 1893 at the World's Columbian Exposition in Chicago.[60]

Susan B. Anthony (1820 - 1906)

> Thus as I passed from town to town was I made to feel the great evil of woman's utter dependence on man for the necessary means to aid reform movements. I never before took in so fully the grand idea of pecuniary independence. Woman must have a purse of her own and how can this be so as long as the law denies to the wife all right to both individual and joint earnings?

There were many women who persevered in the women's rights movement in spite of all difficulties. Susan B. Anthony is the name most often associated with the suffragist movement. Her fame is well deserved for she was the consummate organizer who provided the movement with momentum and direction for half a century. Anthony, however, did not initiate the movement, carry it on single-handedly, nor was she present at the end. Anthony was a relative latecomer to the movement, only becoming interested after meeting Elizabeth Cady Stanton in 1851—three years after the Seneca Falls Convention took place.

Anthony was born in 1820 in Adams, Massachusetts. The family fell on hard times after her father lost his textile mill business, and Anthony turned to teaching—one of the only occupations open to women and one in which the men earned several times a woman's. Her father was an ardent abolitionist, and it was through him that she met Frederick Douglass and other prominent anti-slavery leaders. At one time, she tried working as a paid agent for the temperance society, but withdrew after meeting a great deal of prejudice against women's equal participation, including being told, "The sisters were not invited here to speak!"

It was not long thereafter that Anthony met Amelia Bloomer and Elizabeth Cady Stanton and became committed to women's suffrage. Her first campaign, in 1854, was to initiate a drive to collect signatures for a petition to be presented to the New York legislature. The petition boldly asked for women to be able to control their earnings, custody of their children in divorce, and the right to vote. Anthony used several new political strategies, which established her as an astute political tactician. She chose 60 women, one from every county in the state, to serve as "captains" and collected six thousand signatures in just 10 weeks, a remarkable amount for this period in U.S. history.

Women in 1852 rarely traveled alone, conditions for all but the most affluent traveler were primitive, and finding food and accommodations were almost an overwhelming daily task. In addition, most doors were slammed in their faces as the resident women's husbands "protected" them. Although that campaign was not successful, it did lay the groundwork for legislation in 1860 that gave women the right, in addition to owning property, to collect their own wages, to sue in court, and to have similar property rights at their husband's death as the latter had when his wife pre-deceased him.

Early in the Civil War, Anthony helped organize the Women's Loyal National League that urged emancipation. After the war, she campaigned unsuccessfully to have the language of the Fourteenth Amendment allow for female as well as "Negro" suffrage. In 1866, she became the corresponding secretary of the newly formed American Equal Rights Association. In 1868, she became publisher, and Stanton editor, of a new periodical, *Revolution*. In May 1869, she and Stanton formed the National Woman Suffrage Association of which she remained the principal leader and spokeswoman.

To test the legality of the Fourteenth Amendment, she cast a vote in 1872 in the presidential election in Rochester, New York. She was arrested, convicted and fined, although she refused to pay the fine, and the fine was not enforced. She traveled constantly to campaign for female suffrage in the state referenda that were held around the country. In 1892, two years after the merger of the National and the American into the NAWSA, Anthony became president. Carrie Chapman Catt became her principal lieutenant in later years.

By the 1890s, she had become a national heroine, outliving the abuse and sarcasm that had been directed at her in earlier years. Susan B. Anthony died in 1906, after becoming ill during the annual suffrage convention at which she had told the assembled women, "Failure is impossible." She remained committed to and active in the women's suffrage movement up to the time of her death. In 1979, she became the first woman to be depicted on U.S. currency.[61]

Josephine St. Pierre Ruffin (1842-1924)

> Our woman's movement is a woman's movement in that it is led and directed by women for the good of

women and men, for the benefit of all humanity, which is more than any one branch or section of it.

Josephine St. Pierre Ruffin was an African-American woman who was active in public affairs and an ardent suffragette. Ruffin, a New Englander by birth, had a mixed ancestry of Indian, French, English, and African, and was born of free parents. She also had a relatively genteel upbringing. Nevertheless, she was faced with the same discrimination when it came to education as that of any African-American children. To escape the segregated schools in Boston, her parents sent her to Salem, Massachusetts, where no such color barriers existed.

When she married George L. Ruffin, the young couple decided to live in England to escape discrimination. They returned to America after the outbreak of the Civil War. Her husband enrolled at Harvard Law School to become one of its first African-American male graduates. George Ruffin also was among the first African Americans to serve on the Boston Common Council and to sit on the Massachusetts bench.

Josephine Ruffin became a leader in organizing African-American women's clubs. The Women's Era Club that she organized was among the first African-American women's organizations. She edited *The Woman's Era* newsletter. She also became the first of her race to become a member of the New England Women's Club. She held a respected place in the African-American community and spread her ardent reform views. In 1895, Ruffin convened and addressed representatives of 20 African-American women's clubs and challenged them to form a national organization. They did, in fact, organize the National Federation of Afro-American Women at a national meeting in Boston. Within a year, a merger had been successful with the Colored Women's League of Washington and a new organization formed, the National Association of Colored Women. Ruffin was elected first vice-president. For many years, clubs from around the country joined the organization, and it was a leading force in the African-American community. The continued resistance of all-white national women's clubs reinforced her commitment to the importance of the African-American women's club movement.

Ruffin also was active in the Massachusetts School Suffrage Association and worked closely with other New England women in the suffrage movement, including Lucy Stone and Julia Ward Howe.[62]

Anna Howard Shaw (1847 – 1919)

> Nothing bigger can come to a human being than to love a great cause more than life itself.

The Reverend Dr. Anna Howard Shaw was born in England and came with her family to the U.S. in 1851. Her formative years were spent in Massachusetts on an isolated frontier farm near Big Rapids, Michigan. At age 12, she cleared the farm land, planted crops, and cared for her family as her father was absent, and her mother had had a nervous breakdown. She received a year or two of schooling and, at age 15, became a teacher in a frontier schoolhouse.

In 1870, Shaw preached her first sermon and was licensed to preach in 1871. She graduated in divinity studies from Boston University in 1878. After several rejections, her application for ordination was finally granted in 1880. She began medical studies at Boston University in 1883 and became a lecturer for the Massachusetts Woman Suffrage Association in 1885. In 1886 she received her M.D. degree from Boston University. She opted not to practice medicine, but instead turned to the speaking circuit where her principal themes were temperance and female suffrage. A meeting with Susan B. Anthony in 1888 led her to work for the National. In 1891, she became a national lecturer for the merged NAWSA and from 1892 to 1904 she was vice-president of the organization. In 1904, she became president of the NAWSA, succeeding Carrie Chapman Catt. She served in that position until 1915.

In April 1917, Shaw was named chairman of the Woman's Committee of the United States Council of National Defense. In recognition of her contributions in that position, she received the highest civilian

Presidential citation, the Distinguished Service Medal, the first woman to receive this honor. When she left this position in 1919, she intended to return to the lecture circuit on behalf of the pending suffrage amendment, but former President Taft and the president of Harvard were able to convince her to lecture instead on behalf of President Wilson's League of Nations (the predecessor to the United Nations) plan. She fell ill during the midst of a highly successful speaking tour and died in 1919.[63]

Carrie Chapman Catt (1859 - 1947)

> It is because of the differences between men and women that the nineteenth century more than any other demands the enfranchisement of women.

Carrie Lane was born in Wisconsin and grew up in Iowa. She graduated from Iowa State University at the top of her class, having worked her way through school by washing dishes, working in the school library, and teaching. She was the only woman in her graduating class. After college she worked first as a law clerk, then as a teacher and school superintendent (one of the first women in the nation to be so appointed). Her first husband, Leo Chapman, died of typhoid fever only a few months after their marriage while seeking to get them established in San Francisco. After his death, she worked as San Francisco's first female newspaper reporter before returning to Iowa where she worked as a professional writer and lecturer for the Iowa Woman Suffrage Association.

She shortly became the group's recording secretary and from 1890 to 1892, she served as the Iowa association's state organizer. In 1890, she married George Catt, a successful engineer and supporter of suffrage and his wife's part in the movement. In 1890, she also began working nationally for the NAWSA, speaking in 1890 at its Washington, D.C., convention. In 1892, Susan B. Anthony asked her to address Congress on the proposed suffrage amendment.

Catt proved her mettle in the unsuccessful and grueling South Dakota referendum in 1890 and the successful Colorado referendum in 1893. She became chair of the Organization Committee of the NAWSA where she developed a flair for planning, detail, and seeking out and training fresh leadership. She was instrumental in laying the organizational foundation for the NAWSA in such matters as plans of work for local groups, state headquarters, a manual of organization, a consistent membership system, and sound association finances. In 1900, she succeeded Susan B. Anthony as president of the NAWSA.

After four years, Catt resigned the presidency of the NAWSA and turned her attention first to health matters in her family and then to the cause of international suffrage. In 1904, she helped found the International Women Suffrage Alliance and served as its president until 1923.

In 1915, Catt returned to the U.S. after eight years as IWSA president promoting equal-suffrage rights worldwide. She reassumed the presidency of the NAWSA which had badly splintered under the leadership of Anna Howard Shaw. In 1916, at a NAWSA convention in Atlantic City, New Jersey, Catt unveiled her "Winning Plan" to campaign simultaneously for suffrage at the state and federal levels. Under her leadership, the NAWSA won the backing of the House and Senate and by 1919, the Nineteenth Amendment had been passed by both houses of Congress and sent on to the states for ratification.

Catt founded the League of Women Voters after ratification of the Nineteenth Amendment. She served as its honorary president for the rest of her life. In her later years, Catt's interests broadened to include the causes of world peace and child labor. She founded the National Committee on the Cause and Cure of War in 1925 and supported the League of Nations (which later became the United Nations).[64]

Ida Wells-Barnett (1862 – 1931)

> Is there no redress, no peace, no justice in this land for us? Tell the world the facts.

Ida Wells-Barnett, an African-American journalist from Memphis, Tennessee, was a strong advocate of the suffrage movement and was also concerned with other vital race-specific issues. Ida Wells was born in a small town in Mississippi to slave parents six months before the Emancipation Proclamation. Her parents and three of her siblings died during an epidemic of yellow fever, leaving Ida, at the age of 14, the task of raising her four remaining siblings. Similar to many other women of her generation, she found a teaching position by claiming to be eighteen.

While a journalist, Wells-Barnett decided to combat the recurring incidents of mob lynching in the South that generally went unchallenged in the American press. Her first step was to compile statistics of individual lynchings for 1892 to 1894. She later published a book, *The Red Record*, based on her findings, with an introduction by Frederick Douglass. Wells-Barnett's anti-lynching crusade succeeded in focusing both national and international attention on this alarming situation, but did not endear her to the general American public. She did, however, gain popularity in Great Britain where she was invited to lecture and organize anti-lynching parties.

Wells-Barnett's anti-lynching work in America led to the formation of African-American women's organizations. The first was founded in 1892. White women's clubs also were flourishing during this period. Wells-Barnett saw the potential in combining efforts for the mutual benefit of both groups. Her vision of solidarity was not acceptable to the white women club leaders, however, and her appeal for cooperation made no headway. The white women leaders underscored their rejection during a convention of the General Federation of Women's Clubs. They denied the credentials of the only African-American delegate, representing a leading African-American women's club. Ironically, this treatment was reminiscent of the kind of treatment given women during the World Anti-Slavery Convention in London in 1840.

Wells-Barnett experienced other episodes of racial discrimination even within the suffrage movement. For instance, she had planned to march with the Chicago contingent in the suffrage parade during President Woodrow Wilson's inauguration in 1913. She was told that Southern women in the march would not agree to interracial participation, and she would have to march with the "colored delegation." Wells-Barnett refused to go along with this. So she disappeared from view until after the parade was underway, then stepped from the sidewalk into the line of marchers, flanked on either side by white supporters, and proudly walked the entire parade route without incident.

Wells-Barnett served as secretary of the National Afro-American Council from 1898-1902 and founded and became first president of the Negro Fellowship League in 1920. She was militant in her demand for justice for African Americans and in her insistence that it was to be won by their own efforts. Although initially supportive of the National Association for the Advancement of Colored People, she later distanced herself from its activities.[65]

Mary Church Terrell (1863-1954)

> I have recorded what I have been able to accomplish in spite of the obstacles which I have had to surmount. I have done this, not because I want to tell the world how smart I am, but because both a sense of justice and a regard for truth prompt me to show what a colored woman can achieve in spite of the difficulties by which race prejudice blocks her path if she fits herself to do a certain thing, works with all her might and main to do it and is given a chance.

Mary Church Terrell was born to former slaves in Memphis, Tennessee. After graduating from Oberlin College where she opted for a rigorous four-year "gentlemen's course" to disprove then-widespread theories of racial inferiority, Terrell taught school and became the first African-American woman to serve on the District of Columbia Board of Education. She later earned a master's from Oberlin as well. Terrell was representative of the newly emerging college-trained African-American women, who ardently supported woman's suffrage. She was a featured speaker at national suffrage conventions when African-American women were welcomed as partners in the movement.

Terrell was very bright; she electrified the International Council of Women meeting in Berlin in 1904 when she addressed the assemblage in English, German, and French. Terrell later became the first president of the National Association of Colored Women, following a merger with the National Federation of Afro-American Women. The co-founder and president of the latter organization was Margaret Murray Washington, the third wife of the famed educator and founder of Tuskegee Institute, Booker T. Washington.

During World War I, Terrell worked for the War Risk Insurance Bureau and became involved in a protest about the treatment of African-American women. After her husband's death in 1925, Terrell became increasingly militant in both her politics and her political strategy; she joined picket lines and advocated direct action to challenge discriminatory laws and practices. She sued after being refused readmission to the Washington branch of the American Association of University Women and was eventually admitted to the national body. She was involved in a suit by the Coordinating Committee for the Enforcement of District of Columbia Anti-Discrimination Laws that sued restaurants who refused to serve African Americans. Terrell lived to celebrate the 1954 decision of the U.S. Supreme Court, *Brown v. Board of Education*, which held that segregation of public schools was unlawful. She received honorary doctorates from Howard, Wilberforce, and Oberlin Colleges, and many awards. Many women's clubs were named in her memory as was a school in Washington, D.C.[66]

Alice Paul (1885-1977)

> The struggle in England has gotten down to a physical fight. Here our fight is simply a political one. The question is whether we are good enough politicians to take four million votes and organize them and use them so as to win the vote for the women who are still disfranchised.

Alice Paul was born in New Jersey and reared in a Quaker home. After graduating from Swarthmore College in 1905, she did graduate work at the New York School of Social Work and lived in the New York College Settlement. In 1906, she went to England for three years to do settlement work. While in England, she was not only jailed three times for her suffragist agitation, she also went on a hunger strike and was subjected to forced feeding. While in England, she continued to do graduate work at the universities of Birmingham and London and received a master's degree in absentia from the University of Pennsylvania.

Paul returned to America in 1910 and, while she was completing her Ph.D. in social work at the University of Pennsylvania, began lecturing to American suffrage groups on the lessons learned by the British suffrage movement. Jane Addams, Anna Howard Shaw, and Lucy Burns approached her in 1912 with the possibility of undertaking work for the Susan B. Anthony amendment. Paul eagerly accepted their proposal and was appointed chairman of the Congressional Committee for the NAWSA in 1912.

After organizing the very successful parade of 5,000 women who marched the day before Woodrow Wilson's inauguration, Paul became disenchanted with what she considered was timid policies on the part of the NAWSA, and in 1913, withdrew to found the Congressional Union for Woman Suffrage, which in 1917 merged with the Woman's Party to form the National Woman's Party. Her militancy in supporting women's suffrage led to her being jailed three more times before the passage of the Nineteenth Amendment.

After passage of the Nineteenth Amendment, Paul devoted herself to seeing the successful ratification of the amendment. Then she went to law school, earning a law degree from the Washington College of Law in 1922, and a master's and doctoral degree from American University in 1927 and 1928. Throughout this time, she continued her activities on behalf of equal rights for women in the U.S. and around the world. She drafted and had introduced into Congress the first equal rights amendment for women in 1923. She continued fighting for equal rights through the League of Nations and throughout the world. Elected chairman of the National Women's Party in 1942, she continued thereafter to work for equal rights, a dream that was partly realized in 1970 when the Equal Rights Amendment (ERA) passed the U.S. Congress (although it subsequently failed to get enough states to ratify). Long considered the elder stateswoman of the feminist movement, she was successful in getting the preamble of the charter of the United Nations to include an affirmation of equal rights of women and men.[67]

Chapter Four
Gaining a Foothold

Introduction

The years immediately following the ratification of the women's suffrage amendment (the Nineteenth Amendment) did not result in significant progress for women in terms of additional rights, additional education, or additional employment opportunities. World War II, which ended 25 years after the suffrage amendment was ratified, provided many opportunities for women to enter the work force. However, once the war was over, the returning veterans took preference over women for jobs and educational opportunities. Women's rights began to receive increased attention in conjunction with the civil right's movement in the 1960s, paralleling the relationship between the abolitionist movement and the women's suffrage movement in the 1800s.

Progression of Women's Rights Before World War II

> The vote alone was not even half a loaf...only a crust, a crumb.
> —Elizabeth Cady Stanton[1]

Women worked many long years to win the right to vote—a goal that was viewed by some as a panacea and by others as a step along a continuum toward equal rights and equal opportunity. Having won the right to vote, however, many activists became discouraged that subsequent progress seemed so slow. In the early 1930s, Emily Newell Blair (an acclaimed author, a nationally known feminist, and vice chairman of the Democratic National Committee), in an article titled "Discouraged Feminists,"[2] wrote:

> Feminism, in this country at least, expressed the desire of women once more to have a part in making the world.... In an age where politics counted less than before, they concentrated first on the effort to get political equality.... What these feminists wanted was not merely a chance to work for some man but a chance to rise to positions of authority so they could again be effective in determining the conditions under which they lived. What these women hoped for was a world in which men and women would work in competition with each other and the best individual win. The sex line was to be dropped and the world become the composite work of individuals of both sexes.[3]

But their hopes were dashed. By the mid-1920s, groups ranging from the moderate League of Women Voters to the more radical National Woman's Party were bemoaning their lack of influence on the national scene.[4]

Contrary to what had been predicted by some of the suffragettes' most strident opponents, women did not end up organizing a political party to elect only female candidates to public office, nor was the country's social fabric destroyed by giving women the vote. The solidarity needed for women to wield political power was missing, and women showed the same tendency as men to divide along party lines. Women did begin to vote in increasing numbers, but their increased appearance at the polls did not match their growth in the total population. Women could not deliver a bloc vote, and comparatively few female leaders were interested in political careers. The nearest women came to flexing their collective political muscle at the federal level was the establishment of the Women's Joint Congressional Committee (WJCC).[5]

The WJCC was formed with a dozen of the largest women's organizations united for the purpose of pressing legislation on Congress. Its targets for political action were a constitutional amendment banning child labor and the Sheppard-Towner Act (passed in 1921) providing federal grants-in-aid to states to promote better infant and prenatal maternity care. Even this loose aggregation of women activists was only effective in the years immediately following the achievement of suffrage and fell apart by the start of the Great Depression in 1929, without having accomplished all of its goals.[6]

Women leaders noted with despair that women were not achieving the economic parity with men that they had hoped for, and questions still were being raised about their intellectual abilities. Because for over 30 years so much time and energy in the women's rights movement had been focused on simply acquiring the right to vote, other issues important to feminists, including marriage, divorce, and economic opportunity had been shelved. These leaders were also greatly disappointed that the new generation of women wanted no part of the women's movement. In fact, they seemed to be either embarrassed by it or steered away from it as an institution that had outlived its usefulness. Thus, for the first decade after its passage, the Nineteenth Amendment appeared to be having little or no impact on the political status of females, and for those who still cared, it proved to be a major disappointment. Organized feminism declined after suffrage was gained, so fewer women were advocating for still unachieved rights.[7]

Progression of Education

Although politically and ideologically the 1920s may have been a disappointment for women, some progress was made on the education front.

The 1920s showed greater promise for women in higher education than ever before. A trend toward more equality in education that had begun 60 years earlier continued. As the percentage of people who attended college grew, so did the percentage of women.[8] The 1920s and 1930s also saw the founding of many more Catholic colleges and two-year women's colleges. The emphasis was on "progressive education" that promoted creativity and independence in the classroom.[9]

By 1930, 4.6 percent of men and 3.1 percent of women over the age of 25 had completed four years of college. The percentage of females among college students had risen from 21 percent in 1870 to 47.3 percent in 1920. Some women were even able to attend graduate or professional schools. Women's representation on college faculties rose to a quarter of the total. While these advances were indeed noteworthy, both female faculty and students were still relegated to the less prestigious and lower paying areas of study. Thus, overt and covert segregation seen in education—and other areas crucial to women's advancement—continued, even as there were significant, intermittent breakthroughs.[10]

Educational institutions, both public and private, could exclude women and/or discriminate against them, if they so chose. Texas A&M University, a public institution, admitted no women until 1963. The University of Virginia, another public institution, admitted women undergraduates to all of its colleges only in 1970. Harvard did not admit women to its law school until 1950. In Harvard's case, women were denied an elite legal education at the school considered the best in the nation. A law degree from Harvard was a ticket to a Supreme Court clerkship, a partnership in a prestigious law firm, a Cabinet Post, or even the Supreme Court bench itself.[11]

Although some advances in education and subsequent employment were made by women in the 1920s, progress was curtailed during the Great Depression of the 1930s. Men were given preference in higher education and employment because they were seen as the primary breadwinners.[12]

In general, women lost ground in terms of education relative to men during the years between World War I and World War II. However, some women from minority and working-class groups were able to realize minimal gains. Mother Marie Joseph Butler established the Marymount School in Tarryton, New York, that by 1919 had developed into a college for Catholic women and became a leader in Catholic higher education for the modern world. Sister Madeleva Wolff, third president of St. Mary's College, provided new graduate and undergraduate opportunities for women.[13]

African-American women also benefited to some degree during the interwar period. Many confidently pursued higher education in larger numbers than males, knowing that jobs awaited them as teachers in segregated schools. They also had as advocates a new generation of African-American educators like Lucy Diggs Slowe, dean of women at Howard University. Slowe, dean from 1922 until her death in 1937, began in 1933 to emphasize the importance of education for all women and advised African-American women in particular to study economics and government to have the knowledge necessary to improve the social conditions of all African-American people. She and other educators joined distinguished older colleagues like Nannie Burroughs, who opened the National Training School for Women and Girls in Washington, D.C., and who formed the National League of Republican Colored Women, and Mary McLeod Bethune, who founded the Daytona Literary and Industrial School for Training Negro Girls in Florida and served as an advisor to four presidents, to increase the equality of education for African-American women.[14]

Progression in Employment

The increasing number of women entering college and earning doctoral degrees was a positive sign of change. The number of female professionals also increased, rising from 11.8 percent in 1920 to 14.2 percent in 1930. But most of these female professionals were concentrated in teaching and nursing. By 1930, the percentage of female lawyers and architects remained stable at three percent. In the whole country, there were only 60 female CPAs and 151 dentists. In New York, female professionals included 63,637 teachers and 21,195 nurses, but only 11 engineers and seven inventors. The percentage of women doctors declined from six percent in 1910 to five percent in 1920 and to 4.4 percent in 1930. The absolute numbers fell from 9,015 in 1910 to 6,825 in 1930. Reasons for this decline include a quota on the number of women admitted to medical schools, a limit on the number of female interns accepted, the closing of many of the women's medical colleges, the "professionalization" of medicine, the lack of women in key medical administrative and decision-making positions, and outright hostility toward female students.[15]

Academic women made few gains. While women earned 33 percent of the graduate degrees granted, they occupied only four percent of the full professorships. The percentage of women on college and university faculties peaked in 1930 and declined dramatically until later in the century. A survey of academic women in 1929 concluded that experience contributed little to the advancement of women in academia.[16]

Emily Blair wrote of the despair that pervaded this period by quoting Dr. Anna Howard Shaw:

> You younger women will have a harder task than ours. You will want equality in business and it will be even harder to get than the vote, for you will have to fight for it as individuals and that will not get you far. Women will not unite, since they will be competitors with each other. As soon as a woman has it for herself she will have entered the man's world and cease to fight as a woman for other women.[17]

Blair made the point that men who belonged to the chamber of commerce were bankers, presidents of factories, owners and managers of large companies, lawyers and doctors. These men and these organizations were the economical and political decision makers. The male members of the chamber earned between $5,000 and $50,000 annually. Women were not encouraged, nor did they feel comfortable, joining these types of groups, but those who joined the business and professional women's clubs were predominantly stenographers, clerks and teachers, with an occasional doctor or lawyer. In stark contrast, their average earnings ranged between $750 and $5,000 per year.[18]

World War II Impacts on Women's Rights

World War II saw unprecedented numbers of women enter the work force. Three million females who had never worked before took jobs outside of the home. Women who had been working at low-paying jobs in restaurants, laundries, and retail stores took advantage of the labor shortage to move to high-paying factory jobs. "Rosie the Riveter" became a national heroine. Even professional women were able to break down a few of the barriers because of the extreme shortage of men. The number of women pursuing higher education increased dramatically as the men went off to war. African-American women, in particular, benefited during this period. Although a few had earned doctorates before World War II, more women became the first African-American woman in their fields to earn doctorates and most taught at African-American colleges, where they worked hard to improve instruction.[19]

The war, however, was an emergency situation, and many traditional attitudes toward women reverted post-war. Although legislation was introduced in the Senate to provide for federally subsidized daycare, it died in committee after being referred to the House. In addition, the National War Labor Board (NWLB), established in 1942 by President Roosevelt to determine procedures for setting labor disputes, did not follow through on a commitment to equal pay for equal work, in spite of the principle it had established in three cases of equal pay for equal work for women in the war industry. Women in manufacturing in 1945, for example, still earned only 65 percent of what men did, the same disparity that prevailed in 1940. Instead, the NWLB provided employers with a series of loopholes, e.g., the requirement for equal pay for equal work did not apply to jobs that were "historically" female, or to which women alone were assigned. As a consequence, separate job categories along sex lines continued as before.[20]

Other familiar forms of discrimination continued during the war despite the urgent need for human resources. Women in business and industry were denied the opportunity to hold top management positions, and although there was a critical shortage of physicians, the Army refused to commission female doctors until 1943. One of the clearest indications that there had been little change in traditional attitudes was the government's lack of response to the need for childcare as increasing numbers of mothers entered the work force. Despite a great deal of rhetoric, the federal government made little genuine effort to correct the situation.[21]

After the war ended, the impact on educational opportunities for women significantly declined. Many of the men returning from the war took full advantage of the G.I. Bill, formally known as the Servicemen's Readjustment Act of 1944, that provided federal aid to veterans, particularly in the area of education. The next decade was to reflect this downturn, so that by 1950, women earned only one-fourth of all bachelor's degrees, their lowest share since statistics became available in the 1920s. Women's share of doctorates fell from 18 percent to ten percent between 1930 and 1950, and their share of faculty positions dropped from 32 percent to 23 percent over this same period. For these reasons, the period from the end of World War II until 1960 is viewed as a regression in women's education.[22]

Despite massive layoffs of women after the war, the number of working women did not decline permanently. By 1947, female employment had reached wartime levels and was setting new records in the economic boom of the late 1940s and early 1950s. Most of these jobs, however, were lower-paying jobs in traditionally female fields, and wage discrimination continued as before. Wherever women constituted more than 50 percent of the labor force in an industry, its wages fell below the national wage average.[23]

Although the absolute number of women going to college increased, they constituted a smaller proportion of the total enrollment than before the war, due to the large numbers of men pursuing a college education in response to the G.I. Bill. Labor statistics for 1960 show that the percentage of women in the professions continued to decline from 15 percent in 1930 to eleven percent in 1960, reflecting both the influx of returning veterans and the fact that women no longer had the support of an organized feminist movement nor a coherent feminist ideology. The number of female lawyers and school superintendents decreased. A cap on the number of female admissions to medical school continued, and 70 percent of all hospitals rejected female interns. Although 25 percent of all government workers were female, only three percent held high-level positions. A 1946 survey by *Fortune* magazine showed that 53 percent of the business executives interviewed had little confidence in women's ability to handle management positions, while 66 percent said that women were less able than men to make decisions.[24]

While a revolution occurred in female employment in the 1940s and the 1950s in terms of the number of wives and mothers entering the work force, there was no corresponding shift in attitudes toward women by the general public. Most Americans still subscribed to the idea that women's proper place was in the home. Although most of the women who worked did so out of necessity to raise the family above the poverty level or to reach middle class comfort, and not solely for individual fulfillment, there seemed to be a commonly held idea that the wife's job was temporary until some indeterminate time when it would no longer be necessary. In other words, women did not seek careers; they sought jobs.[25]

There was a large gap between the perception that women didn't need to work and thus didn't need to be paid equally or be treated equally and the large number of women who were actually in the work force. However, this gap between reality and societal attitudes did not spur a rise in feminism. Unfortunately, for most women, employment outside the home simply meant holding two jobs instead of one. Despite the growing numbers of working mothers, there was little demand for childcare centers or other forms of community support. A few die-hards still advocated passage of the Equal Rights Amendment (ERA); however, even women leaders like Eleanor Roosevelt maintained that protective legislation was more important than the abstract principle of legal equality.[26]

The attitude toward marriage and careers from 1945 to 1960 is reflective of the social environment of that time. The average age of marriage for American women dropped to its lowest level. The birth rate soared, especially among the college educated. And even among this group, marriage took precedence over careers. There was a strong ideological reason for this change in attitude. Despite the fact that so many women had entered the work force during World War II, men and women were coming to the conclusion that women could not combine families and careers. Given such a stark choice, most women opted for a family.[27]

As time progressed, fewer and fewer females earned the highest professional degrees. In the 1920s and early 1930s, 14 percent had been granted the Ph.D. This percentage decreased to ten percent in 1950. A mass white exodus to suburbia began, and for the first time, college-educated, middle class women had as many children as poor women did.[28]

The "honeymoon" with suburbia was not to last, however. Despite the ideological climate that emphasized the importance of marriage and family that drove many well-educated wives to the suburbs in the 1950s, this idealistic picture changed dramatically in the 1960s. An increasing number of college-trained women were finding less and less contentment from an exclusive diet of domesticity, and once again entered the work force. The percentage of college-educated females who worked outside the home increased from seven percent in 1950 to 25 percent in 1960. Two years later, 53 percent of all female college graduates were employed, and 70 percent who had five or more years of higher education worked outside the home.[29]

What was most startling about this renewed revolution in female employment was that many women found that they were receiving more gratification from their jobs than they did from their domestic roles. In one survey reported at the time, two-thirds of those who responded said it was their jobs that made them feel important and useful, but at the same time they felt guilty for feeling this way. Thus began the era of dual-role conflict that Betty Friedan, a feminist largely credited with beginning the late-twentieth-century women's rights movement and founder of the

National Organization for Women, was to label the "problem without a name."[30]

The Advent of the New Feminism

A number of factors could explain the dramatic rebirth of the women's movement in the early 1960s—the first serious resurgence of feminism since the 1920s. Most historians agree it was a combination of forces that came together quite explosively. And, certainly, discontented, educated suburban housewives were ready for a new perspective on life. Then, too, Betty Friedan and Gloria Steinem, a journalist who started *Ms.*, a successful feminist magazine, appeared well-equipped to provide a new approach for women and to serve as their heroes.[31]

Friedan's book, *The Feminine Mystique*, broke through the complacency of the 1950s by launching a blistering attack on "suburban America" and the status and roles it assigned to women. Friedan's book was not intended to be a theoretical treatise on the "dismal plight" of women. It was meant to be a "call to action," and it worked. It succeeded in arousing women—mostly middle-class and white—in a way that nothing else had for generations. Gloria Steinem's bohemian way of life, and her fervent activism on the part of women, also stirred women's emotions and strengthened their resolve to begin to take charge of their own lives.[32]

There were other dynamic forces at work in the 1960s that influenced the rebirth of feminism. For one, the McCarthy era had ended. During that infamous period, anyone who showed a sign of nonconformity, or questioned the status quo, was quickly labeled a Communist. The infamous "witch-hunt" trials resulted in countless numbers of Americans being "blacklisted" and their careers placed in jeopardy. By the time Friedan's book appeared, this threat was gone, and the middle-class women she appealed to were in a less conservative frame of mind. Consequently, they were more receptive to radical ideas that promised a freedom they felt had been denied.[33]

A second vital force was the civil rights movement, which was at its peak in the 1960s. Just as the birth of feminism had been closely associated with the abolitionist movement in the mid-nineteenth century, so was its rebirth in the twentieth century closely related to the struggle for racial equality. The militancy of college students during the 1960s mirrored some of the rebellious activism so prominent during the suffrage movement. The students protested on campuses and in the streets, and traveled to the South on behalf of civil rights.[34]

Paving the Way Politically

The 1960s was an eventful period in women's history. One of the most significant, and controversial, occurrences was the publication of the report of the Presidential Commission on the Status of Women. The first of its kind, the Commission was the brain-child of Esther Peterson, whom President John F. Kennedy had appointed director of the Women's Bureau in the Labor Department in 1961.

The Commission, established in 1961, was charged with investigating and suggesting remedies for "prejudices and outmoded customs [that] act as barriers to the full realization of women's basic rights." Eleanor Roosevelt chaired the commission, and Peterson served as the executive vice-chair. Seven committees representing various facets of American life—civil and political rights, education, federal employment, private employment, home and community, social security and taxes, and protective labor legislation—were involved in the commission's work, and their final report (issued in 1963) proved that in almost every area, women were second-class citizens.

The many criticisms of the report included its ambivalence about women's proper sphere. On the one hand, it emphasized women's unique and unchangeable role as wives and mothers. On the other, it maintained that obstacles to women's full participation should be removed. Another criticism of the report was its moderate tone, which had been significantly stronger in the initial report. The Commission's actions led to two immediate announcements by President Kennedy in 1962:

1) Women were to be on an equal basis with men for Civil Service promotion, and
2) All executive department promotions were to be based on merit.

The Equal Pay Act, signed in June 1963, and the creation of the Interdepartmental Committee on the Status of Women, also resulted from the report.[35]

Equal Pay Act

Shortly after publication of the Commission's report, Congress passed the Equal Pay Act, and President Kennedy signed it into law in June 1963. The act was sponsored by Representative Edith Green of Oregon, one of the most influential members of Congress at the time. It was the first major piece of legislation addressing sexual inequality since the Nineteenth Amendment. At the time the legislation was passed, working women earned only 59 percent of the average income earned by men.[36]

The Equal Pay Act, which amends the Fair Labor Standards Act, reads, in part, "...no employer shall...discriminate...between employees on the basis of sex by paying wages at a rate less than the rate at which he pays wages to employees of the opposite sex for equal work...the performance of which requires equal skill, effort and responsibility, and which are performed under similar working conditions." The Equal Pay Act does allow employers to discriminate between workers regardless of sex under four conditions:

1. If the determination of pay is based upon a system of seniority
2. If differentiation is based upon a merit system according to predetermined criteria
3. If calculations are based upon differences in quantity or quality of production

4. If the differential is based on any other factor other than sex.[37]

Thus, to determine whether or not an individual is being discriminated against in violation of the Equal Pay Act, one must compare the jobs and job responsibilities of the individuals and not the individuals themselves. Because the Equal Pay Act is part of the Fair Labor Standards Act, it contains strong remedies for violations; for example, employees who prevail in a lawsuit against an employer are entitled to recover any wages that would have been paid had they not been discriminated against. Employees are also entitled to recover compensatory damages, unless the employer is able to show that he or she "acted in good faith," and had reasonable grounds for believing that the Act was not violated. Successful plaintiffs can also recover attorney's fees incurred in filing lawsuits.[38]

The Equal Pay Act applies to all employees, including business executives and professionals who would normally be exempt from minimum wage and overtime compensation. The Act also covers state and local government employees, unless they are specifically exempted from its coverage.

Most feminists consider the Equal Pay Act the most effective of all the legislation passed to eliminate sex discrimination in employment. One key reason was that the very existence of the law had a salutary effect on businesses and institutions that had never been under review, nor ever had to defend against complaints.[39]

Civil Rights Act—Title VII

In 1964, a major piece of legislation—Title VII of the Civil Rights Act—was passed to prohibit discrimination in employment on the basis of race, religion, color, national origin, and sex by private employers, unions, employment agencies, and colleges and universities. The bill specifically excluded federal, state, and local governments. The original intent of the bill was to deal with racial inequality. The amendment adding the word "sex" was proposed by the powerful chair of the House Rules Committee, Howard Smith of Virginia, in an effort to retard its passage.

Smith urged Congress "to protect our spinster friends in their 'right' to a husband and family," a conniving plea that was met with roars of laughter.[40]

> If there were any need to prove your disrespect you've already proved it by your laughter. We've sat here for four days discussing the rights of blacks and other minorities and there has been no laughter, not even a smile. But when we suggest that you shouldn't discriminate against your own wives, your own mothers, your own granddaughters, your own sisters, then you laugh.[41]

> Better if Congress just abolished sex itself. A maid can now be a man. Girl Friday is an intolerable offense...[42]

His apparent intent was to burden the entire law with the addition of gender and cause the defeat of the entire law due to the expected ensuing controversy and ridicule. Thereafter, his strategy of adding "sex" was referred to as a "joke." Nonetheless, the amendment to the language was retained, and the law was passed.[43]

The Equal Employment Opportunity Commission (EEOC) was formed to enforce Title VII. Much to the surprise of the first chairman of the Commission, Franklin D. Roosevelt, Jr., the EEOC was deluged with complaints from women, rather than racial minorities. Considering the levity with which the word "sex" was added, it is not surprising that the first executive director of the Commission described this trend as a "fluke...conceived out of wedlock." The rigorous enforcement of women's complaints was not considered a high priority issue, and the enforcement procedure remains long and cumbersome to this day. The full implementation of the law has remained a major concern of feminists throughout the years since Title VII's passage. One clear benefit of Title VII, however, is that it opened the door to affirmative action.[44]

National Organization for Women (NOW)

One of the new feminist organizations organized as an outgrowth of the 1960s and serving as the harbinger of the new feminist approach was the National Organization for Women (NOW). NOW was founded in 1966 by Betty Friedan and other women convening in Washington, D.C., for the National Conference of State Commissions on the Status of Women. NOW describes itself as a civil rights organization to bring women into "truly equal partnership with men" in all areas of American society. Through its political arm, it lobbies for women's rights and disseminates feminist ideology. It often is credited with being the first women's group in the twentieth century to combat sex discrimination in all spheres of life: social, political, economic and psychological.[45]

NOW's 1968 Bill of Rights covers every conceivable kind of equality for women. It calls for support of the Equal Rights Amendment, enforcement of laws banning sex discrimination in employment and allowing maternity leave rights and social security benefits, tax deductions for home and childcare expenses for working parents, childcare centers, equal and unsegregated education, equal job-training opportunities, and the right of women to control their reproductive lives.

At the time, most Americans considered the NOW platform to be quite radical because it linked the issues of economic equality to the necessity of providing government support. Not surprisingly, many younger women at that time did not think it was radical enough in its analysis and approach. Many of the young women who joined the movement during that period had come from the radical student and civil rights groups of the early 1960s. Some of them felt the organization's concentration on legal remedies would lead to the same kind of stalemate situation that the suffragists faced in 1920. Others were disdainful of what they considered the middle-class and reformist character of the new feminism.[46]

Equal Rights Amendment

Written by Alice Paul in 1921 (then a leader of the National Women's Party), the Equal Rights Amendment (ERA) to the Constitution was first introduced into the Congress in 1923 as a way to legally and universally upgrade the status of women. The amendment, first called the Lucretia Mott amendment, reads, "Equality of rights under the law shall not be denied or abridged by the United States or any State on account of sex." The history of the ERA has been fraught with disappointment, defeat, and divisiveness. Initially, the proposed amendment attracted little support from women's groups because it was associated with extremist feminist views. The first group that decided to support it was the National Women's Party, which had supported suffrage but opposed protective legislation.[47]

Most suffragists followed the lead of the National Consumers' League—the powerful advocate of protective legislation. They opposed the ERA because they believed that it would endanger the so-called protective laws (limitations on the number of hours women could work, required minimum wages for women, and requirements for working conditions). During the 1930s, other women's groups began to support the ERA. The large majority of ERA supporters were well-educated, middle-class women. By 1944, the platforms of both major parties supported the amendment, probably in response to women's efforts during World War II.[48]

By the 1960s, some prominent female leaders who had been long-time opponents of ERA began to change their positions. Protective labor legislation for women was no longer as high a priority as it had been. This obviously had an effect on one eminent former suffragist who had been a strong opponent of the ERA. Shortly before her death, Eleanor Roosevelt wrote, "Many of us opposed the amendment because we felt it would do away with protection in the labor field: Now with unionization, there is no reason why you shouldn't have it if you want it."[49]

After its first introduction in 1923, the ERA was re-introduced at each successive session of Congress—primarily as a symbolic gesture—until

February 1970. At that time, a group of militant activists from the newly reinvigorated woman's movement, including members of NOW, whose bill of rights demanded passage of the ERA, pushed for hearings. Their campaign paid off. In May 1970, the ERA passed 354 to 15 in the House, and on March 22, 1972, by a vote of 84 to 8 in the Senate. At the time the Senate approved the ERA, a time limit of seven years was set for ratification.[50]

By the original seven-year deadline set by Congress—March 22, 1979—only 35 states had ratified the ERA; three states short of the necessary thirty-eight. Congress then extended the deadline until June 30, 1982. However, at the date of expiration, the ERA was still three states short of the number needed for ratification.[51]

Opponents of the ERA usually based their arguments on their commitment to the "family values" concept. Anti-ERA activists, such as Phyllis Schlafly, a lawyer who headed the Stop-ERA campaign, accused supporters of rejecting family, wifehood, and childrearing in favor of adopting lifestyles patterned after those of male professionals. Opponents warned that if the ERA were ratified, it would lead to increased hardships for wives and mothers: the breakdown of the family, the failure of husbands to provide financial support, and the failure of employers to pay heed to women's special needs. This latter argument probably had the strongest effect in diluting women leaders' support of ERA, at least as long as protective legislation remained at the forefront of women's concerns. Ironically, the policies that had kept women from competing for certain jobs—such as bans on women doing night work—had begun to be overruled by federal courts as early as 1969.[52]

Although it appears that the defeat of the ERA was a result of a conflict between women who were professionals and women who were homemakers, in fact the polls between 1972 and 1982 showed that public support for the ERA never dropped below 50 percent and rose to as high as 63 percent of the general public. However, legislative outcomes do not always follow public sentiment. In the end, the ERA was defeated by a minority. Most American state legislators supported it, but supporters were successful in getting only 35 of the required 38 states to ratify the amendment.[53]

Just how significant was the defeat of the ERA to the feminist movement? At least one historian claims that it could not have brought about the radical changes that opponents so feared and that proponents expected. Feminism has not died, although the desirability of a gender-neutral policy is still being debated. And, in spite of the fact that the ERA was defeated, many of the outcomes expected after its passage have happened anyway—the divorce rate has risen dramatically, poverty has become a condition of primarily women and children, and working mothers remained burdened by scarce and inadequate child care.[54]

The legislative developments of the 1960s not only awakened the issue of equality between the sexes from its dormant state, but also refueled the resurgence of organized feminism. The 1960s and 1970s feminists continued the suffragette's struggle and made significant progress, but it is clear that there are still more battles to fight.

KEY WOMEN OF THIS PERIOD

Mary McLeod Bethune (1875-1955)

> Invest in the human soul. Who knows, it may be a diamond in the rough.

Mary Jane McLeod was born in South Carolina, the fifteenth of 17 children. Scholarships enabled her to attend Scotia Seminary (now Barber-Scotia College in Concord, North Carolina) and Moody Bible Institute in Chicago. She married Albertus L. Bethune in May 1898.

They moved to the east cost of Florida where a large African-American population had grown up at the time of the construction of the Florida East Coast Railway. In 1904, Bethune founded the Daytona Educational and Industrial School for Negro Girls in Daytona Beach,

Florida. She worked tirelessly to build the schoolhouse, solicit help and contributions, and enlist the goodwill of the African-American and white communities. Bethune was able to expand the school to a high school, then a junior college, and in 1923 it merged with Cookman Institute to become what was known from 1929 forward as Bethune-Cookman College. Bethune remained president of the college until 1942 and resumed the position in 1946 and 1947 before retiring as president emeritus.

An advisor to four presidents, she worked to attack discrimination and increase opportunities for African Americans. She served on the National Child Welfare Commission as an appointee of President Coolidge and later President Hoover. President Hoover also appointed her to the Commission on Home Building and Home Ownership. After receiving the Spingarn Medal of the National Association for the Advancement of Colored People in 1935, she was appointed as administrative assistant for Negro Affairs of the National Youth Administration by President Franklin D. Roosevelt. In 1935, she founded the National Council of Negro Women, of which she remained president until 1949. She advised Roosevelt on minority affairs and the Secretary of War on the selection of officer candidates for the Women's Army Auxiliary Corps. President Truman appointed her to the Committee of Twelve for National Defense. She was the recipient of numerous awards and honorary degrees.[55]

Esther Peterson (1906 – 1997)

> I think we helped move the women's question up so it's beginning to be equal with the men's question. We're not in the basement anymore.

Esther Peterson was a powerful catalyst for change throughout her life—for the labor movement, for the women's movement, and for the consumer movement. She was the first special assistant to the president for consumer affairs when she assumed that position under President

Lyndon B. Johnson. Prior to that service, she was at the Women's Bureau, where she served as Director from 1961 to 1964. While in the Department of Labor, she also served as assistant secretary of labor for labor standards. Her efforts were instrumental in creating the President's Commission on the Status of Women, of which she served as vice-chair, and the passage of the Equal Pay Act of 1963. The Commission marked the first time that federal attention was focused on the status and condition of women in the workplace. From 1964 to 1967, she was chair of the President's Committee on Consumer Interests.

Peterson served President Jimmy Carter again in the position as special assistant for consumer affairs. During his administration, she also chaired the Consumer Affairs Council, designed to give consumers a voice in federal policy making. The Food Marketing Institute named an annual award after her—the Esther Peterson Award—for the person who does the most for consumers. President Jimmy Carter awarded her the Presidential Medal of Freedom in 1979.[56]

Betty Friedan (1921 -)

> Some worry that we'll lose our femininity and our men if we get equality. Since femininity is being a woman and feeling good about it, clearly the better you feel about being yourself as a person, the better you feel about being a woman. And, it seems to me, the better you are able to love a man.

Betty Friedan has been central to the reshaping of American attitudes toward women's lives and rights. Her 1963 book *The Feminine Mystique* brought to the national consciousness the roles and pressures on women to perform solely as wives and mothers. It was an outgrowth of a questionnaire that she circulated to her fellow Smith College alumnae, many of whom, like her, had become dissatisfied with their roles as housewives. The public discussion that followed the publication of the book was bolstered by her lectures and television and radio appearances around the country.

Friedan was a founder of the National Organization for Women, of which she served as president. While she was president of NOW, she directed campaigns for the ending of sex-classified employment notices, for greater representation of women in government, for childcare centers for working mothers, for legalized abortion, and other reforms. She was also a convener of the National Women's Political Caucus, and led the nationwide Women's Strike for Equality. Friedan was an essential leader in the struggle for passage of the Equal Rights Amendment. In 1973, she became Director of the First Women's Bank and Trust Company.

She has published several books, received the Eleanor Roosevelt Leadership Award in 1989, and co-chaired Women, Men, and Media, a gender-based research organization that conducts research on gender and the media.[57]

Gloria Steinem (1934 -)

If the shoe doesn't fit, must we change the foot?

A leading figure in the women's rights movement of the late 1900s, Steinem is an activist and change agent, dedicated to fashioning a world that fits the needs of its people. The granddaughter of a suffragette, Steinem graduated from Smith College in 1956, and went to India on a scholarship. While there, she participated in nonviolent protests against government policy.

Steinem began working in journalism in 1960, publishing articles in such magazines as *Vogue*, *Glamour*, and *Cosmopolitan*. She gained attention in 1963 with the article, "I Was a Playboy Bunny" that told of her experiences as a waitress at Hugh Hefner's Playboy Club. In 1958, she began writing a column called "The City Politic" for *New York Magazine*. Steinem's involvement with feminism intensified in 1968 when she attended a meeting of a radical feminist group, The Redstockings.

In 1971, Steinem helped found the National Women's Political Caucus with Betty Friedan and others. That same year, she helped produce the first issue of the feminist magazine *Ms*. In 1972, Steinem helped found the Ms. Foundation for Women, which raises funds to assist underprivileged girls and women. Throughout the 1970s and 80s, Steinem focused much of her attention on political organizations. She is a founding member of the Coalition of Labor Union Women, Voters for Choice and Women Against Pornography. Her publications include *Outrageous Acts and Everyday Rebellions* (1983), *Revolution from Within* (1992) and *Moving Beyond Words* (1994).[58]

Chapter 5
Making Progress

Introduction

During the last 25 years of the twentieth century, women's rights in the U.S. have continued to move forward in fits and starts. Key pieces of legislation (some of which were amendments to landmark acts passed in the 1960s) have contributed to the long-term advancement and quality of opportunities for professional women. Other federal actions, including executive orders and rulings of the U.S. Supreme Court, also have had a significant impact on the advancement of women's rights. High visibility events such as the appointments of Sandra Day O'Connor and Ruth Bader Ginsburg to the U.S. Supreme Court and Anita Hill's testimony during the Clarence Thomas Supreme Court confirmation hearings have brought much attention to the progress—and lack of progress—made by women during the twentieth century. Women's advancement in the professions and the workplace has without question been propelled forward by the many legislative actions. Media attention to the legislation and the follow through, or lack of follow through, by corporations and organizations has placed the subject of gender equity on the forefront of the public's consciousness.

Federal Actions

The Equal Pay Act (1963) and Title VII of the Civil Rights Act (1964), two landmark pieces of legislation in the early 1960s, substantially furthered the progress of women. During the rest of the century, amendments to previous acts, executive orders from the President, and rulings of the Supreme Court continued the progression. It is important to understand that many of the liberties and rights we take for granted now were only recently instituted as law.

The Dawn of Affirmative Action

In September 1965, President Johnson essentially began affirmative action by signing Executive Order 11246. The Order required all companies who wanted to do business with the federal government not only to provide equal opportunity for all but also to take affirmative action (defined as extra steps) to bring their hiring in line with available labor pools by race. This action was taken in large measure due to continued occupational segregation by race, especially in the skilled trades. After this order, affirmative action was required for all companies—whether or not they had been proven to have discriminated. Those companies that had discriminated and had been sued were already required as part of their court settlements to take steps to compensate for previous practices. Now, with Executive Order 11246, workers began to get protection from covert racial discrimination regardless of whether their organization had been proven to have discriminated or not.[1]

Recognition of Sex Discrimination

Two years later, in 1967, President Johnson signed Executive Order 11375, extending Executive Order 11246 to include "sex" as a protected category. This executive order now required that affirmative action be taken on behalf of women in addition to minorities (as required by Executive Order 11246) so that hiring was in line with gender proportions as well as racial proportions in the relevant labor pools. Feminist activists, who were just getting organized, recognized that the ability of the federal government to award or withhold funds (often called the "power of the federal purse") could be used to rectify past unfair hiring practices with regard to women and heavily lobbied President Johnson to sign this Executive Order.

The academic labor pool was one of the first to be tapped. The Office of Federal Contract Compliance (OFCC) in the Department of Labor was responsible for enforcement of these executive orders. However, the OFCC did not seem particularly eager to deal with women's issues, particularly when minority issues were viewed to be much more pressing and women were being discriminated against in different occupational sectors than minorities.

During President Nixon's administration, Bernice Sandler, an officer of the Women's Equity Action League (WEAL) and a psychologist who had personally experienced employment discrimination, decided to test the reach of Executive Order 11375 specifically with regard to universities. Would the OFCC rule that universities that did "business" (i.e., received research funding) with the federal government be required to have an affirmative action plan?

On January 31, 1970, WEAL filed a class action suit against over 250 universities and research institutions under Executive Order 11375 for race and sex discrimination in program, personnel, and admissions policies. The Office of Federal Contract Compliance ruled that the universities and research institutions did have to comply. The OFCC found that patterns of employment in the nation's colleges and universities did not reflect the existing labor pools of women. This ruling was particularly significant because up until that point, these institutions had considered themselves exempt from executive orders. This ruling changed the manner in which universities did their hiring across the entire institution and opened up many more opportunities for women and minority faculty and postdoctoral appointments.[2] It also forced the OFCC to confront at least some of the issues related to sexual discrimination in various occupational sectors.

Gaining Equality in Higher Education

Until the late 1960s, there were no legal remedies available to women for sex discrimination in higher education.[3] The Fourteenth Amendment to the Constitution, that assures all persons equal protection of the law, was interpreted as being applicable to racial, but not sexual, discrimination. Title VII of the Civil Rights Act of 1964 prohibited discrimination in employment, but did not apply to educational institutions. And it exempted state and local governments, so students and employees in public schools and colleges were not protected.

After WEAL filed another lawsuit in fall 1970 against every medical school in the United States for sex discrimination, Congress finally became convinced of the need to strengthen Title VII of the Civil Rights Act. Action culminated in the passage of several pieces of legislation: the Equal Employment Opportunity Act of 1972, amendments to Title VII of the 1964 Civil Rights Act, and Title IX of the Education Amendments of 1972.

The Equal Employment Opportunity Act of 1972 was particularly important for education, as institutions of higher learning were deemed no longer exempt from compliance with employment discrimination. The 1972 amendments to Title VII of the 1964 Civil Rights Act overturned the exemption from discrimination compliance for state and local government employers. The 1972 amendments also gave the Equal Employment Opportunity Commission (EEOC) the power to initiate cases of discrimination itself. Prior to these amendments, individuals needed to bring discrimination charges before the EEOC or the federal courts. As amended, Title VII does not apply to employers of fewer than 15 workers, Indian tribes, or religious bodies.[4]

Title IX of the Education Amendments of 1972 prohibited discrimination on the basis of sex in all federally assisted educational programs. It also extended both Title VII and the Equal Pay Act to educational workers, and empowered the attorney general to instigate suits against institutions. While it was being debated, Representative Edith Green discouraged feminists from lobbying too publicly for the bill, lest attention be paid to its potentially wide-ranging powers.[5] It declared, in part, "No person in the United States shall, on the basis of sex, be excluded from participation in, be denied the benefits of or be subjected to discrimination under any education program or activity receiving federal financial assistance."[6]

Title IX specifically applies to admissions of females to all public undergraduate institutions, professional schools, graduate schools, and vocational schools, including vocational high schools, that admit students of both sexes.[7] A very significant consequence of this act was that caps on the admission of female students to medical, law, business, and other professional schools were finally abolished.[8] The law exempted from its coverage admissions to elementary and secondary schools, private colleges, and religious organizations. As was made apparent in the 1980s and 90s furor over the admission of females to military schools, these institutions were also exempt, specifically because they were single-sex institutions.[9]

Title IX covers almost all areas of student life and activities, including financial aid, athletics, housing, services provided to students, and rules governing the visiting privileges of members of the opposite sex in campus dormitories. The most intense opposition to Title IX arose in the area of male varsity athletics. Here the issue was equal or proportionately equal funding for school-based sports for women. Indeed, by the end of the twentieth century, Title IX had, in most people's minds, become synonymous with equal access for women to participate in college athletics.[10]

Regulations issued in 1975 under Title IX required colleges and universities to conduct self-evaluations of institutional policies and procedures for possible discriminatory effects, and to take remedial measures to ensure compliance with the law. Upon finding discrimination under Title IX, affirmative action programs can be required by court order.[11]

Title IX has ended up being a very powerful tool for gaining equal opportunity in higher education. Any institution that wants or already does receive federal money—whether public or private college, graduate or professional school—can not hold women to higher standards than men, and vice versa. It prevents discrimination against married women, pregnant women, or mothers of young children—all of which occurred prior to its passage. And—most innovative of all—Title IX mandates equal opportunity for women athletes.

Title IX has been found to be indispensable in overcoming overt discrimination within the general rules and procedures of colleges and universities. Official policies no longer sanction restrictive practices against women in college admissions, financial and student services, residence hall rules, and athletics. Pat Schroeder, former congresswoman from Colorado, applauds Title IX for giving college women a menu of choices, but she also points out that there is no Title IX equivalent in the workplace. When women enter the job market, they often discover discrimination is still alive and well.[12] And, of course, there is still not equal funding for men's and women's college sports.

Opening Up the Bank Coffers

The Equal Credit Opportunity Act, enacted in 1974, prohibited credit discrimination on the basis of sex, race, marital status, religion, national origin, age, or receipt of public assistance. The legislation was viewed as providing a leg up to women attempting to borrow money to start or expand a business. Prior to the passage of this legislation, women were denied loans that a man was granted to run a comparable business, simply because they were women. Married women had a particularly difficult time obtaining credit. NOW was very involved in this piece of legislation and positioned it as a fairness issue to broaden support. And NOW became very active after the passage of the act to insure that the Federal Reserve Board, which was responsible for writing the necessary implementing regulations, did so in a manner favorable to women and without undermining Congress' original intent, apparent in the initial draft of the regulations.[13]

Other Legislative Action Barriers Fall

In 1972, the Equal Pay Act was expanded to cover professional and administrative employees for the first time. The State and Local Fiscal Assistance Act of 1972, which instituted revenue sharing, prohibited recipients of funds from discriminating in the use of those funds. Discrimination in employment was prohibited based on race, color, sex, religion, national origin, age, and physical handicap under the provisions of this Act.[14]

Sexual Harassment Regulations

Sexual harassment, either overt or subtle, had been a bane of women in the workplace for many years. For much of that time, many corporations and managers either refused to acknowledge that there was a problem or blamed women for being "too sensitive." In 1980, the Equal Employment Opportunity Commission (EEOC) determined that women probably weren't being too sensitive and issued regulations defining sexual harassment as a form of sex discrimination and thus prohibited under the Civil Rights Act of 1964. Significant U.S. Supreme Court rulings in the 1980s and 90s have further defined which situations constitute sexual harassment and what actions employers need to take to prevent sexual harassment of employees, be they male or female.[15]

In October 1991, the confirmation hearings of Clarence Thomas for the United States Supreme Court brought the issue of sexual harassment to the forefront of Americans' thoughts. In 1991, Anita Hill, an African American like Thomas, was a professor of law at the University of Oklahoma. But from 1981 to 1983, she had worked for Thomas at the Department of Education and had followed him as his special assistant to the EEOC. Anita Hill's allegations that she had been sexually harassed while a subordinate of Clarence Thomas' caused many Americans to question the definition of sexual harassment as well as its pervasiveness in the workplace. Nonetheless, Thomas was confirmed, and a significant percentage of the public believed his version of the events, particularly in view of Hill's silence about the harassment for nearly a decade.[16]

In 1992, when reports of the Navy's Tailhook scandal surfaced, many people began to learn more about sexual harassment and believed that Hill may have been telling the truth after all. In September 1991, the Tailhook Association held its annual symposium and convention in Las Vegas, Nevada, for military aviators. During this convention, unsuspecting female guests, including 14 female Navy officers, were attacked, groped, grabbed, and handled by a throng of male Navy aviators. One of these women, Lieutenant Paula A. Coughlin, aide to Rear Admiral John Snyder, subsequently filed suit against the Tailhook Association as well as the Las Vegas Hilton, alledging that the "gauntlet" to which she had been subjected had been in existence at these conventions for many years and that both the Las Vegas Hilton and senior military leaders had been aware of this behavior. Coughlin eventually resigned from the Navy.[17] But the issue of sexual harassment had now been elevated to a much higher level.

Civil Rights Restoration Act

Title IX was able to extend the federal reach to bar sex discrimination in higher education only to those programs at institutions that could be categorized as "federally assisted educational programs." Most higher education institutions, whether private or state-supported, receive federal funds in support of research grants and contracts. All receive federal aid through their students' federally guaranteed student loans. By the 1980s, people started to wonder whether or not educational equity for women was assured in programs not directly funded by the government.[18]

In 1984, Grove City College decided to find out the answer to that question. The Supreme Court ruled in favor of the college saying that only those programs that received federal funding were required to provide educational equity. In response to this ruling, Congress enacted the Civil Rights Restoration Act of 1987, which includes any program or activity of or in an institution, agency or corporation that receives federal assistance. Compliance with the act requires the institution, agency, or corporation to assure compliance also with Title IX, Title VII, the Age

Discrimination Act of 1972, Section 504 of the Rehabilitation Act of 1973, and Title VI of the Civil Rights Act of 1964. Although President Reagan vetoed the Civil Rights Restoration Act, there was sufficient Congressional support for it, and both the House and Senate overrode his veto on March 22, 1988. This act exempts private, and some public, undergraduate institutions that had been continuously and traditionally single-sex. Private and public military institutions were also still exempted.[19]

Women in Positions of Power in Government

Despite these legislative advances, women were slow to gain a physical presence in any of our three branches of government—executive, legislative, and judicial. To date, key decisionmakers in the executive branch all have been male, although Geraldine Ferraro ran as the Democratic vice-presidential candidate in 1984. Representatives and senators comprise the decision-making roles in the legislative branch.

Jeannette Rankin was the first woman elected to the U.S. House of Representatives in 1917. She was elected as a Republican from Montana and served in the Sixty-fifth Congress (1917-1919). Rebecca Latimer Felton, a Democrat from Georgia, served two days in the U.S. Senate in 1922, having been appointed on a largely symbolic basis. The first woman elected to the Senate was Hattie Wyatt Caraway, Democrat from Arkansas, who was elected to a term after first having been appointed in 1931 to fill the vacancy caused by the death of her husband. For the Congress that was seated in January 2001, 13 senators were female and the House of Representatives included 59 women, both record highs. Having a woman on the Supreme Court, the most powerful decision making body in the U.S., was a goal of feminists for many years. Their efforts were finally rewarded in 1981 when Sandra Day O'Connor became one of the nine Supreme Court justices.[20]

Sandra Day O'Connor, the first woman on the Supreme Court, was named to the Court by President Reagan. Her career path exemplifies the difficulties even the best and brightest women have had to undergo. She had terrible difficulties finding even entry-level positions after law school, simply because of her gender. Ruth Bader Ginsburg, the second female Supreme Court Justice nominated by President Clinton in 1993, experienced many of these same difficulties.[21]

Progress in Education

Women have made significant achievements in education since 1970. These advancements came as the result of a confluence of forces that revolutionized American education. This revolution included the *Brown v. Board of Education* decision, which outlawed racially segregated schools; subsequent movements for bilingual and multicultural education; Title IX of the Education Amendments of 1972; and the revitalized feminist movement. Both individually and as a group, women were persistent in filing complaints to keep the pressure on public institutions, designated enforcement agencies, and the courts. In addition, existing colleges and universities were expanded, and a network of community colleges came into being. The result of these changes was the opening of new educational and career opportunities for women of all backgrounds.[22]

Brown decision. *Brown v. Board of Education of Topeka, Kansas*, was decided by the U.S. Supreme Court in 1954. Linda Brown had been denied admission to her local elementary school in Topeka, Kansas, because she was African American. The Supreme Court unanimously overruled the separate but equal doctrine of *Plessy v. Ferguson*, which had been in place since 1896, and held that segregation of public schools was unlawful.[23]

This action was significant both for advances in racial equality and for women's rights. The U.S. Supreme Court had determined that "the plaintiffs and others similarly situated for whom the actions have been brought are, by reason of the segregation complained of, deprived of the equal protection of the laws guaranteed by the Fourteenth Amendment." That amendment reads in part, "No State shall make or enforce any law which shall abridge the privileges or immunities of citizens of the United States;

nor shall any State deprive any person of life, liberty, or property, without due process of law; nor deny to any person within its jurisdiction the equal protection of the laws."

The decision provided a tremendous impetus to the civil rights movements of the 1950s and 60s that resulted not only in the Civil Rights Act of 1964 (that prohibited discrimination in employment on the basis of sex) but also in the Equal Pay Act. The Brown decision hastened the end of segregation in all public facilities and accommodations, not just in education.[24]

Bilingual and multicultural education. Minority women began to see increasing opportunities in education and employment as a result of the legislation previously discussed. The resurgence of bilingual education and an awareness of America's multicultural society in the late twentieth century opened up additional opportunities. Minority women began to be especially active in the movements for civil rights and cultural pluralism.

The Bilingual Education Act of 1968 passed as a result of the energized civil rights movement and growing immigration. It provided federal funding to encourage local school districts to try approaches incorporating native-language instruction. The landmark *Lau v. Nichols* case (decided by the Supreme Court in 1974) required schools to take affirmative steps to overcome language barriers impeding children's access to the curriculum. The principle of equal education was endorsed by Congress through the Equal Educational Opportunity Act of 1974. This act recognized that identical education does not constitute equal education under Title VI of the Civil Rights Act of 1964.[25]

Minority women were now able to take advantage of educational opportunities and make their marks in the educational field and in the professions.[26]

Enrollment Increases. A spectacular gain in female participation in higher education has been seen as a result of the civil rights movement in the 1960s and resulting legislation. Between 1970 and 1986, women earned a majority of all bachelor's and master's degrees, and during this period women's share of doctorates increased from 13 percent to 35 percent. The 1995 figures on total fall enrollment of women in institutions of higher education are an encouraging sign of their continuing progress in attaining equality in education. Women comprised 55.8 percent of the total undergraduate enrollment, 55.7 percent of the graduate enrollment, and 41.6 percent of first-professional-degrees enrollment.[27]

The 1970s and 80s saw significant gains in the college enrollment rates for African-American women in particular. During the early 1970s, their representation began to increase marginally, but remained lower than four percent of the total college population. The next decade, however, African-American women's enrollment rates rose from 66 to 82 percent to those of white women and from 42 to 82 percent of those for white men. Less information was collected on other minority women for earlier years, so trends are difficult to assess. The upward trends in increasing enrollment for women continued through the end of the twentieth century.[28]

Also, particularly noteworthy was the dramatic inroads women made into the study of law, business administration, medicine, and theology during the 1970s. Law schools saw a dramatic influx of women. However, the greatest change was seen in medical schools, where quotas had long been the sanctioned practice. Between 1964 and 1973, the number of female medical students increased 138.6 percent. In 1974, women constituted 16 percent of total enrollment in law schools. Women represented only 6.8 percent of the graduating class from medical schools in 1965, as compared with 10.7 percent in 1974. During the latter year, just under 20 percent of the total enrollment in medical school was female.[29]

The increase of women engineering students and graduates rose most dramatically from the early 1970s to the mid 1980s, although the overall numbers still remained low. In 1972, the percentage of women receiving bachelors degrees in engineering finally reached 1.2 percent. By 1987, the level had reached 15.4 percent.[30] On the other hand, women remained disproportionately represented in the traditionally female fields of study such as teaching, social work, nursing, and library science.

Women's representation on faculties and in administrative positions in colleges and universities began to grow during this period, although equality continued to remain elusive. Women faculty, as well as female students, remained disproportionately concentrated in community colleges and other less prestigious educational institutions rather than in research universities. Although women may receive more degrees than men in a few fields, they are not in control in their professions in any field other than nursing. Men continue to hold the preponderance of senior faculty and administrative positions—even in traditionally female areas of study. Men also hold most of the leadership positions in the professional associations in these fields.[31]

Nevertheless, women are reaching higher levels of education in greater numbers than ever before, allowing them to make significant inroads into professional careers.

Women's Studies

As important as the other advances that women have made in higher education since 1970 is the introduction and growth of women's studies as a formal area of teaching and research. Relatively unknown prior to 1970, women's studies was introduced on a few campuses experimentally by a few feminist scholars. An extensive effort has been made since its humble beginnings to incorporate women's studies into the core curriculum, and to a limited extent, this goal has been accomplished.

Since the 1980s, women's studies courses have been available on many campuses, either as courses within existing disciplines or as an interdisciplinary field of study. Its popularity is evidenced by the fact that more than 30,000 courses are being offered by colleges and universities throughout the country. In addition, formal degree programs in this discipline have become widespread, and their numbers are growing. A network of women's studies research centers and institutes have had a direct influence on public policy as well as on the academic curriculum.

Women's studies courses and programs are even making their appearance abroad, not only in Europe but also in developing countries.[32]

Non-Traditional Students

Another recent development that has had an impact on women in education has been the influx of re-entry (older and returning) women into institutions of higher learning. In fact, in the 1960s, colleges and universities found themselves increasingly confronted by a student body that did not fit into the customary mold. Students—both men and women— were increasingly older, with family and career responsibilities, and an interest in part-time study. And most entered or re-entered for the express purpose of furthering their career goals. Between 1966 and the mid-1980s, the number of part-time students increased 150 percent.[33]

By 1970, colleges and universities had alternative delivery systems in place to respond to the phenomenal increase in the part-time student population. "Weekend colleges," for example made it possible for adults who needed to study part-time, or off-campus, to earn their degrees. Adult degree programs were pioneered as early as the 1950s by Columbia University, Brooklyn College, and the University of Oklahoma. The development of the College Proficiency Examination Program and the College-level Examination Program make it possible to measure competencies of students gained through forms of study other than formal courses. Thus, "assessment degrees" can now be earned by an adult who qualifies, and he or she does not have to expend the time formerly required in degree programs. This development has been especially significant for women, who often have domestic and work responsibilities in addition to school.[34]

Current Role of Education

The critical question is what role education plays in women's continuing quest for equality, especially within the professions. It is an indisputable fact that there has been a phenomenal gender shift, with women becoming the growing majority on campuses nationwide. This has led to a rather ironic twist, as some schools have stopped just short of instituting "affirmative action for men." A number of colleges are now concerned about how deeply they must dip into their pool of male applicants to fill an incoming class proportionately. This shift could be viewed as an amazing success story in women's history.[35]

In the 1998 academic year, women earned over 57 percent of all bachelor's degrees, compared with 43 percent in 1970 and less than 24 percent in 1950. This upward trend is expected to continue. The National Center for Education Statistics projects that by 2007, female college enrollment will have reached 57 percent, and the number of bachelor's degrees awarded to women nationwide will have reached 58 percent. The U.S. Department of Education projects that women will outnumber men in undergraduate and graduate programs by 9.2 million to 6.9 million by 2008.[36]

What has caused this gender-pattern shift in college enrollment? Theories abound. One of the most popular is that men see more opportunities in the existing robust economy to land good-paying jobs without a college degree. Some of these opportunities are imagined, but others are very real, as unemployment is at a low point, and the pay high in the technology industries, for example. Two-thirds of the people entering the information-technology industry are male. In the 1990s, computer companies became so desperate as to actively recruit high school seniors—mostly male.[37]

Comparing total lifetime earnings by level of education clarifies the picture. Individuals without a high school diploma can expect to earn around $608,000 in an average lifetime; high school graduates, $820,000; those with associate degrees, around $1,000,000; bachelor's degree recipients, over $1,400,000; those holding a master's degree, over $1,600,000; and doctorates, more than $2,000,000. In other words, as the title of a 1990s article on the work place put it, "Education Pays!"[38]

At least some of our graduating high school students must realize that there is a strong connection between education and expected earnings. According to the U.S. Bureau of Labor Statistics, two-thirds of 1997 high school graduates enrolled in colleges or universities the following fall—up from 62 percent for 1995 graduates. Two-thirds of the new college students signed up at four-year colleges, and the other one-third enrolled at two-year colleges.[39]

Although women are succeeding in enrolling in college and securing their undergraduate degrees at levels not seen previously in U.S. history, some concern remains about the areas that women choose to study. Women tend not to select engineering or science, including computer science, and this lowers their projected lifetime earnings as compared to men. The areas of study preferred by women, such as English over engineering, or psychology over computer science tends to reinforce their lower-tier position in the economy. Women are still a minority in graduate business school as well, although numbers of women pursuing medical and law degrees have reached a par with men.

Although women may not be pursuing technical educations in great numbers, they still may be preparing themselves in large measure for ascension to management jobs, even in the high-tech industry. Education and communication skills seem to be the key to job opportunities in management. Thus women holding a degree of any type have demonstrated their capacity to learn and apply knowledge. In many instances, employers are realizing that skills can be learned on the job, and this has resulted in an increased demand for liberal arts majors as management trainees in a variety of industries. Some fields actually seek their managers among recent college graduates. These management positions can prove lucrative. In the hospitality industry, for instance, managers at national chains such as Chili's restaurants, Marriott hotels and even McDonalds can earn up to $50,000 a year, and more with bonuses.[40]

The differences in post-secondary paths between men and women might do more to foster gender equality than constitutional amendments or court decisions. With women gaining an edge in education, they could increasingly move into positions of power in all aspects of society. These positions would allow them to personally close the salary gap, and potentially increase the number of women in the top tiers of organizations. Managers do not necessarily need technical expertise; but they do need leadership ability and the capacity to see the "big picture"—and college can provide this. If, however, technical education will be a requirement in the future for large number of corporate executives, women will need to study those fields in larger numbers than is currently the case.[41]

Progress in the Work Force

Once women land a job, however, they are not treated as equals with men. The most obvious and indisputable discrepancy is in pay. An earnings gap has existed for many years between men's average earnings and women's average earnings. In 1973, women who worked full-time earned only 57 percent of men's full-time earnings. Of all the high-paying jobs (which at the time were those paying greater than $15,000 per year), 94 percent were held by white males. The remaining six percent were divided between minority men and females of all races.[42]

Despite much controversy in the mid to late 1990s over affirmative action, women and minorities still have not reached pay equity with men. An editorial in a February 1996 issue of *Glamour* asked the question: "Are Women Equal Yet?" The article lists 18 reasons why women still need affirmative action. These include:[43]

- A woman working full-time, year-round, will make on average only 72 cents for every $1 a man makes.

- For an executive, the ratio is 74 cents. For a retail clerk, the ratio is 66 cents. And, if she is a woman of color, the ratio is 63 cents.

- When women go into traditionally male occupations, they are paid less than men (female truck drivers, 70 cents; female lawyers, 74 cents). When men go into traditionally female professions, they are paid more than the women (registered nurses, $1.04, male office clerks, $1.09, male cashiers, $1.17).

- A man with a college degree will make an average of $15,000 a year more than a similarly qualified women—a difference that translates into $600,000 more in income over a 40-year career.

- If women continue to move into the top business ranks at the current rate, the numbers of male and female senior managers will not be equal until the year 2470.

- Teachers in kindergarten through 12th grade are 73 percent female. Only 35.5 percent of principals and just 10.2 percent of school superintendents are women.

- In 1994, 24,505 sex discrimination complaints were filed with the U.S. Equal Employment Opportunity Commission—a 28 percent increase since 1991.

- According to the National Council for Research on Women, females are three times more likely than men to lose a job because of sexual harassment, five times more likely to transfer to another job to escape it, and nine times more likely to quit because of it.

- Woman-owned businesses receive less than two percent of government contracts, yet they employ more than 15 percent of the total U.S. workforce—more than 15.5 million people.

- Interestingly, the Center for Policy Alternatives found in a series of mixed gender focus groups, most women identified inequality as a serious problem in the workplace, in terms of pay and promotions and personal respect. On the other hand, few of the male participants expressed the belief that there were significant inequalities. They saw sexual harassment as the only serious gender-related workplace problem, and their main concern was about unfair accusations against men.

> As Anne Bryant, the executive director of the American Association of University Women (AAUW) points out: "What many people don't seem to recognize is that affirmative action has helped give wives, mothers and daughters a chance to contribute to their families' security. Affirmative action has benefited virtually every family in America."

The women's movement over the years, and the affirmative action programs, have helped to make professional careers a viable choice for women with career ambitions. However, the debate over "feminism" and "affirmative action" continues unabated, and is likely to continue on both issues until well into the new millennium. There are no quick and easy answers as to what is right and what is wrong about either. Their fate depends upon the strength and perseverance of those who believe in the value of feminism and/or affirmative action to achieve that elusive goal that women have been seeking for centuries: Equality.

KEY WOMEN OF THIS PERIOD

Sandra Day O'Connor (1930 -)

> As the first woman to be nominated as a Supreme Court Justice, I am particularly honored. But I happily share the honor with millions of American women of yesterday and today whose abilities and conduct have given me this opportunity of service.

The first woman named to the U.S. Supreme Court, Sandra Day O'Connor, broke the ultimate "glass ceiling" in the legal profession. Born in El Paso, Texas, O'Connor graduated third highest in her class with a law degree from Stanford University in 1952. While at Stanford, she served on the board of editors of the *Stanford Law Review*.

After her graduation, the only job offer O'Connor received was that of a legal secretary in Los Angeles, in spite of her outstanding performance at Stanford. Instead, she entered public service, working in the San Mateo County district attorney's office. O'Connor worked as a civilian lawyer for the Quartermaster Corps while her husband was on military duty in Europe. Upon returning to the U.S., she opened her own small practice. In 1960, after the birth of the second of three sons, she became a full-time homemaker. In 1965, O'Connor returned to work as an assistant attorney general for the State of Arizona, a position she held until 1969. She was named to fill a vacancy in the Arizona State Senate in 1969 and was subsequently re-elected for two two-year terms. During her last term, she served as Senate Majority Leader, becoming the first woman majority leader in any state senate.

In 1974, after a hard-fought election, she won a judgeship on the Maricopa County Superior Court. After declining to run for governor of Arizona against incumbent Bruce Babbitt, she was nominated by Governor Babbitt as his first appointee to the Arizona Court of Appeals in 1979. Nominated by President Reagan, who had during his campaign promised to appoint a woman to the Supreme Court, in July 1981, she was confirmed by the Senate in September 1981 by a vote of 99-0, and sworn in on September 25, 1981.[44]

Ruth Bader Ginsburg (1933 -)

> I pray that I may be all that she [her mother] would have been had she lived in an age when women could aspire and achieve and daughters are cherished as much as sons.

Ruth Bader Ginsburg, second woman to be named to the U.S. Supreme Court, grew up in New York City. The day before her high school graduation in 1950, at which she was scheduled to speak, her mother died of cervical cancer. She attended Cornell University on scholarship and earned a bachelor's degree in government. She then attended the law schools at Harvard and Columbia Universities. At Harvard, she was one of only nine women in a class of over 500 students. Ginsburg was named editor of the *Harvard Law Review* in spite of these odds, before transferring to Columbia University Law School when her husband moved to New York City.

Although she graduated first in her law class in 1959, she was unable to find a job in a law firm as neither mothers nor Jews were being hired. Eventually she found employment as a clerk with a federal district judge in New York. In 1963, she received an honorary degree from the University of Lund (Sweden) for her work there. That same year, she became a faculty member at Rutgers University Law School. Ginsburg also began to take on cases for the American Civil Liberties Union (ACLU) with a particular emphasis in sex discrimination cases. She was the first tenured female professor at Columbia Law School (1972). She later became the general counsel to the ACLU, where she was known for exposing the gender biases of existing laws when she presented her arguments.

In 1980, she was appointed to the U.S. Court of Appeals for the District of Columbia Circuit by President Jimmy Carter. In 1993, President Bill Clinton nominated Ginsburg to the Supreme Court. She took the oath of office on August 10, 1993.[45]

Geraldine Ferraro (1935 -)

> Tonight the daughter of an immigrant from Italy has been chosen to run for vice president in the new land my father came to love...

Geraldine Ferraro was the first woman to be nominated by any major political party as its candidate for vice president of the United States. The daughter of Italian immigrants whose father died when she was eight years old, Ferraro attended Marymount College in Manhattan on a scholarship. She majored in English and graduated with a bachelor's degree in 1956.

She taught English in public schools in Queens while attending the Fordham University Law School at night. She earned her law degree in 1960, passed the New York bar exam that summer, and then married John Zaccaro a week after passing the bar.

During the next 14 years, she was involved somewhat in local politics, but was primarily focused on raising her three children. In 1974, when her youngest child entered school, she accepted a position as assistant district attorney in the Investigations Bureau in Queens. In 1974, she transferred to the Special Victims Bureau, which she had helped to create to handle cases of rape and domestic violence.

She successfully ran for the U.S. House of Representatives in 1978 from New York City's 9th District as a Democrat. Her platform supported law and order, the elderly, and neighborhood preservation. She was reelected in 1980 and 1982. While in the House, Ferraro was elected secretary of the Democratic caucus and took a seat on the House Steering and Policy Committee. In 1984, she was appointed chair of the Democratic platform committee, the first woman to hold the post. In 1984, Ferraro was selected as the vice-presidential candidate on the Democratic ticket with former Vice President Walter Mondale. Mondale lost the presidential election to Ronald Reagan.

She has written an autobiography, *Ferraro: My Story* (1985) and has actively campaigned on behalf of female political candidates, held a fellowship at the Harvard Institute of Politics (1988), and unsuccessfully run for the U.S. Senate in 1992. Her additional books include *Changing History: Women, Power and Politics*, and *Framing a Life: A Family Memoir* (with Catherine Whitney).[46]

Chapter 6
Battling Still

Introduction

> Getting Even: Why can't a woman be paid like a man? We examine the great salary divide - and what you can do to bridge it.
> — *Working Woman*
> (July/August 1999)

> Timing is Everything: Academe's Annual Baby Boom. Female professors say they feel pressure to plan childbirth for the summer.
> — *The Chronicle of Higher Education*
> (June 25, 1999)

> Minority women report obstacles.
> — *Denver Rocky Mountain News*
> (July 14, 1999)

The women's rights movement has made many advances since women won the right to vote in 1920. Yet, as the above headlines from 1999 indicate, many battles are still being fought, with mind-numbing regularity.[1] Issues of concern for professional women, and for all women, persist in a wide range of areas including:

- sexual harassment
- advancement and promotion
- equitable compensation
- life/work balance

Many women are starting their own businesses to address these issues and because of the control they then have over their careers and lives.

Sexual Harassment

Though individuals differ on what defines sexual harassment, it is generally agreed that it impacts the ability of women to advance and be taken seriously in the workplace, whether they are in professional, trade, or service-oriented positions. For many years, women did not like to talk about sexual harassment—often because their complaints were not taken seriously—especially if they had been victims of egregious behavior. In recent years, after several high-profile cases gained national prominence, the subject has begun to receive widespread attention. As a result, more women have begun to come forward to file complaints against employers.

The number of companies in which human resources professionals deal regularly with sexual harassment complaints is significant, though it has abated somewhat. A 1998 survey of 900 human resources officials at large companies found that 70 percent of the respondents said they had handled at least one sexual harassment complaint in 1997, whereas in 1995, 92 percent said they had. A big reason for the decrease was that 62 percent of the companies now provide sexual harassment training (up from 34 percent in the previous year).[2] It seems that it has taken multimillion dollar settlements receiving nationwide publicity to prompt public focus on actually remedying sexual harassment issues in the workplace.

But what exactly is sexual harassment, and where is it possible to draw the line? Determining when behavior is or is not harassment has been difficult in the past, and the definition may continue to be elusive. The legal definition of sexual harassment is a kind of sex discrimination, prohibited under Title VII of the Civil Rights Act of 1964. The courts have defined two kinds of harassment. One is *quid pro quo*—a Latin term meaning "this for that"—i.e., you give me something (sex), and I'll give you something (advancement or other favors at work). The other definition is "hostile environment" harassment that can include everything from unwelcome sexual advances to lewd comments. The behavior must create such an intimidating, hostile, or offensive work environment that it interferes with the another person's ability to do his or her job.[3]

Why is this issue of sexual harassment of interest to professional women? Sexual harassment can make the workplace an unwelcoming place, so much so that women become inclined to change jobs and, sometimes, careers. Obviously, these types of changes can have a negative impact on a person's ability to advance within an organization. Recent court rulings have better defined the actions that employees and employers must take with regard to sexual harassment. The Supreme Court in its 1998 ruling noted that it was giving employers "an incentive to prevent and eliminate harassment." Success along these lines would be a very positive development for all employees, particularly, women.[4]

Advancement/Promotion/Glass Ceiling

Over the past several decades, women have made great strides in obtaining entry-level positions, accessing the bottom rungs of their respective professions. Women are now a significant part of the work force. Still, progress has not been as steady for women seeking to move into the upper echelons of management. Whether or not getting to the top is tougher for women remains a controversial issue. Most agree that there is much work to be done before women achieve parity in all aspects of their work lives. Others contend that women can rise to the helm just as easily as men if they have the same qualifications and are willing to work equally as hard.

According to the majority of workers, however, the so-called "glass ceiling" still exists. The Federal Glass Ceiling Commission determined that glass ceilings are the artificial barriers that deny women and minorities the opportunity to advance within their careers.[5] The "glass wall" phenomenon, in which women are denied the diversity of experience necessary to move up the corporate ladder, also is prevalent. These shatter-proof barriers are reflected in the low numbers of women and minorities in top-level positions relative to their numbers in the work force and the length of time they have been in the pipeline. Advancement and promotion for women is slow, as reflected in at least three significant areas of corporate America: in officer positions, in the chief executive officer position, and on boards of directors. This lack of progression into top-level management positions contributes to the wage disparities between men and women.

In 1998, only 63 women (2.7 percent) of the top 2,320 top-earning corporate officers in Fortune 500 companies were women. In July 1999, a woman named Carleton (Carly) Fiorina was made CEO of Hewlett-Packard Company, bringing the number of female CEOs of Fortune 500 companies up to three out of 500. Women on boards of directors of the Fortune 500 now total 671 out of a total of 6,064 board seats, or 11 percent.[6]

Many theories abound as to why women's progress up the corporate ladder has been so slow. One expert offers, "Organizations clearly reproduce themselves. People in power (who are mostly masculine men) mentor, encourage, and advance people who are most like themselves."[7] In other words, men tend to promote individuals in their own image. Often, then, the handful of women who do achieve senior rank usually resemble the men in power. Confronted with the choice of continuing with the same value system as their male predecessors, or using new criteria, many women opt to judge and be judged by the male value system. These women identify with the male-culture orientation of the company or firm, and often deny there is sex discrimination in the workplace and, therefore, fail to mentor other promising women.

Whether women follow the "male model" in developing their corporate image or not, they still are functioning in what is largely a man's world, where many of the rules are the same in the late 1990s as they were in the late 1970s. Whereas men have to work hard, make the numbers, and be a team player if they want to get ahead, women have to work harder, make higher numbers, and prove their team affiliation to get ahead. They also, in many instances, have to do more to stand out—like taking on the tough assignments others shun.[8]

It appears that no matter how committed, nor how much of a team player a woman is, she is often faced with the assumption that she somehow lacks the requisite managerial traits. One recent survey that examined 13 areas of management ability provided significant ammunition to rebut such an assumption. Categories examined in the survey included problem solving, planning, controlling, managing self, managing relationships, leading, and communicating.[9] Women were found to do a better job than men in 28 of 31 key management categories, including keeping productivity high, getting things done on time, problem-solving and planning, and generating ideas. Women were comparable with men in delegating responsibility. The only categories in which women were rated lower were their abilities to handle pressure, cope with their own frustration, and self-promote. The key finding of the survey is that women *do* have the requisite capabilities to be top managers.

The good news is that a growing cadre of women who launched their careers in the 1970s have begun breaking through cracks in the glass ceiling to land top corporate jobs formerly monopolized by men. Research shows that the number of female managers has doubled in the past 20 years, and women entrepreneurs are increasing at twice the rate of male business owners. These success stories give room for optimism but do not mean that American corporations have suddenly become level playing fields after years of white male domination. At the same time, it would be a mistake to ignore obvious evidence that something important is beginning to happen, and a "breakthrough generation" of women is beginning to attain power.[10]

Compensation

Income is the most visible measure of the economic status of women in the professions; historically, there has been a gap between the overall earnings of women and men in the work force. Researchers have examined the factors underlying earning differentials over time, but no matter how the gaps in earning are measured, the disparity remains. *Working Woman* magazine reports that according to the U.S. Census Bureau, in 1999, women earn 74 cents on average to every dollar that men earn.[11]

It is true that the wage gap has closed significantly since President John F. Kennedy signed the Equal Pay Act in 1963. However, significant wage disparities remain. The wage disparity issue stands near the top of the list of issues that most concern working women. A survey of 50,000 working women across the country conducted by the AFL-CIO in 1997 found that one-third of the respondents indicated that their jobs do not provide pay equal to that of their male counterparts. Almost 99 percent of respondents agreed equal pay is an important issue. These findings are reinforced by the 1999 *Working Woman* survey:[12]

- Women earn significantly less than men do for the same work in almost every position of every industry, including those that women dominate, such as nursing and secretarial work.

- Even among top earners, women bring home 68 cents for every dollar earned by men. If the chief executive officers are excluded from the top earners, the ratio only increases to 77 cents.

- At the start of the 1980s, women earned 60 cents to every man's dollar. By 1993, the ratio had increased to 71 cents. In 1999, the ratio had reached 74 cents.

- This disparity exists even though:
  1. Women now represent almost half of all managers and professionals.
  2. Women own nearly 40 percent of all U.S. businesses.
  3. There are two federal laws, an executive order, and numerous state and local statutes forbidding wage discrimination based on sex.

- High-profile sex discrimination lawsuits have resulted in large payoffs to the women who were discriminated against.[13]

In the face of gains made by women in nontraditional professions, equal compensation for comparable work should not be an issue, but it is. The most frequent arguments to explain the disparity include seniority and level of competency.

The basis of the seniority argument is that professional women simply have not been in the work force long enough to have reached the level of compensation of their male counterparts. This is simply not true. Another frequent argument is that women have not attained the same level of competency (as measured by education and experience) as the men in their work environments. This second argument does not jibe at all with the statistics that demonstrate women are getting higher levels of education than men. Some women take time off for family, but many do not. More women are earning college degrees now than men and are on a par with male graduates in medical and law school. This pipeline theory, though frequently put forth, is not the answer; qualified women exist—they are just not being paid or promoted commensurately.

Life/Work Balance

Balance. Work/Life issues. Family. Why are these concerns considered women's issues and not family (and thus everyone's) issues? This is a question that will continue to haunt American society until we come to an understanding that everyone's future depends on reaching the sort of balance in life that will enable all of us to successfully raise children, handle matters related to ill family members, and take care of our aging parents. Men, as well as women, need to ensure that life/work balance issues are addressed.

Over and over, research indicates that women are fed up with fighting to balance work and family. A groundbreaking survey conducted in the late 1990s shows women today are more focused on family and less driven by career goals than at any time in the past two decades. Three parallel surveys, called "Update: Women," have been a barometer of social change in women's attitudes across three decades. Begun in 1979, the researchers report the results of surveys and in-depth interviews with thousands of women over 30 years.[14]

In the late 1970s, working women paid a personal price for their career success with higher divorce rates and less family time. During the late 1980s, women were still trying to do it all, and experiencing "burnout" at an alarming rate as a consequence. The most recent "Update: Women" survey shows a profound social shift has occurred since the 1970s in women's attitudes about life, work, and the struggle to balance both. By the late 1990s, the idealized version of "superwoman" had all but disappeared, and women who have tried to do it all have begun to rebel.

Other recent studies also suggest that women no longer are willing to make unreasonable sacrifices for the sake of a career. Many women appear to be unwilling to play the political games required in many workplace cultures. In frustration, many make different choices about their lives. Many are starting their own businesses; women-owned businesses now account for one-third of U.S. firms, and represent one of the most rapidly expanding sectors of the economy.[15]

Women report that they leave the corporate world for any number of reasons, including the belief that their advancement opportunities are limited. Others are simply tired of the excessive demands of corporate life, which seem to leave little room for anything else. According to recent studies, nearly 60 percent of women with corporate experience said that glass ceiling issues helped push them out of large companies. Most commented that there was nothing that would induce them to return to their former positions. One respondent was quoted as saying, "Women are realizing that there are ways to have it all, and it's much more doable if you're managing your own company."[16]

Even those women who don't choose to go out on their own are seeking a more compatible working arrangement that allows them the option to have both a career and a personal life. Some women elect to work part-time while their children are young. Others make the decision to put their careers on hold for a time, so they can have children. Whatever the decision, women no longer are embarrassed about being either a "stay-at-home" mom or working outside the home and leaving childcare responsibilities to others. They do, however, resent being criticized or penalized for whatever decisions they make.

Despite the once again favorable attitude toward staying home with children, the Bureau of Labor statistics shows there is no mass exodus out of the workplace. The economic reality is that most people, whether in two-parent or single-parent households, need to work throughout their adult lives. As a consequence, the majority of today's mothers are in the labor market. Those women who cannot afford to be "stay-at-home moms" are actively looking for ways to ensure the desired balance between work and family.

Parenting

Like the life/work balance, the issue of parenting is often categorized as a "woman's issue." It is not. It is truly an issue for society. Both men and women are parents; the only way to solve issues of concern in these areas is to work together.

Survey after survey attest to unfair penalties imposed on women in the workplace who decide to have children. Survey respondents cite repercussions for taking maternity leave, serious problems with work reentry after taking maternity leave, and hostile, career-derailing behavior from colleagues and bosses in response to the decision to become a mother. These confining attitudes and behaviors have been described as "micro-inequities."

These small but significant inequalities occur daily in the lives of professional women. At first, they may seem inconsequential, as they often are hidden in the informal communication channels of an organization. Over time, however, they accumulate and may severely constrain a woman's confidence in her abilities and limit her career progress. Many MBAs, lawyers, and physicians claim that micro-inequities compound for the professional woman who chooses to also be a mother.[17]

A woman's visible pregnancy is a constant reminder to her colleagues, bosses, clients, or patients that she has a personal life. Many women acknowledge their pregnancies might create legitimate concerns from colleagues who worry their own work loads might increase, or whose unit's productivity might decline during family leave. They do not, however, agree with the penalties exacted for choosing motherhood. Many professional women reported experiencing a "maternal wall."

One female attorney, who was surveyed about workplace discrimination, commented that when she returned to her law firm after a four-month maternal leave, her boss questioned her commitment to the firm. He pointed to a monthly billing report that highlighted a serious loss of income because of her absence. The attorney noticed the irony that the strong track record she'd had before her brief absence for maternity leave was being held against her. She left the firm to become a sole practitioner because she believed her future with that firm had been irreparably compromised.

Another attorney commented that when she became pregnant, her relationship with some of the firm's partners changed almost immediately. She was an associate at a large firm and worked a typical 60-hour week. Her doctor advised her that working full-time was fine, but full-time to him meant a 40-hour week. She decided to follow her doctor's advice. When she advised the managing partner of her decision, her relationship with him deteriorated rapidly and was never the same, up to the time she finally left the firm.

Women in medicine have their own "war stories" to tell about the difficulties they encountered when they became pregnant, or when they took leave to deal with urgent family matters. One physician reported that she experienced outright misogyny when she used accumulated vacation time to be with a sick child. She was warned that other employees were getting upset about her taking time off, and she had better get back to work quickly.

Dr. Mary Howell, associate dean of faculty affairs at Harvard Medical School from 1972 to 1975, recalls genuine hostility to her pregnancy. "The more pregnant I got, the more invisible I got—because doctors can't be pregnant." Her experiences as dean led her to publish a very strongly worded book based on the survey responses of women medical students across the country titled *Why Would a Girl Go into Medicine? Medical Education in the United States: A Guide for Women* under the pseudonym of Margaret A. Campbell, M.D. These survey results and others reinforce what has been called the theory of "cumulative career advantages or disadvantages: alternatively called the theory of 'limited differences'." Advantages and disadvantages accrued from the early years of one's career onward will accumulate or cascade in importance over time. If, for example, female physicians take time off or slow down early in their careers to accommodate the needs of their families, the long-term effects on their careers versus male peers will be magnified in terms of salary progression, external grant funding, sponsors or mentors, and thus chances for success.[18]

The Family and Medical Leave Act (FMLA), giving pregnant women and mothers (and fathers) added protection, went into effect August 5, 1993. FMLA provides certain employees with up to 12 work weeks of unpaid job-protected leave a year, and requires group health benefits be maintained during the leave. The law applies to all public agencies, schools, and private sector employers with 50 or more employees. Upon return from FMLA leave, an employee must be restored to his or her original job or to an "equivalent" job.[19]

Family Friendly Policies

Both men and women indicate that more flexibility at work would assist them in ensuring a work and family balance. Aon Consulting, one of the world's largest human resources consulting firms, surveyed 1,800 workers, both men and women, and found the number of employees who say they suffer job "burnout" has jumped from 39 percent in 1995 to 53 percent in 1998. What's more, the evidence points to a significant correlation between job stress and loyalty decline. The rise in workplace stress may be related to the finding that the percentage of workers reporting regular 50-hour work weeks has nearly doubled since 1995.

Such data suggest a fairly high "misery level," the study concludes. Workers have so little time for their lives, they devote a percentage of their time at work to personal matters. What employees most desire is recognition of the importance of personal and family time. What seems to matter most now is having time to devote to family and friends, rest and recreation, spirituality, and volunteer work. For some people this means making a radical shift in lifestyle. Some have changed careers in order to downsize their work load. The trade off for most is learning to live on a lower income, which requires sacrifices that not everyone can afford or is willing to make.[20]

Employees have always had families, so what is different about the workplace now? For many years, employees came to work to do their jobs and the motto for corporate America seemed to be, "Leave your troubles at the door!" This, of course, was impossible to do. Worries about kids, elderly parents, and marital problems were always commonplace, but employees endeavored to hide personal issues, and employers conveniently refused to acknowledge their existence.

The reality is that work and family concerns affect employees of both sexes. Clearly the number of women in the workplace has created a need for employers to be flexible, but not just because of the female employees. Parental benefits are sometimes perceived as "special treatment" for women, although many fathers are beginning to express similar concerns about their own parenting responsibilities. The message that needs to get through is that the issue of work/life balance is no longer solely "a woman's issue."

In those companies that provide it, comprehensive "family friendly" programs include child- and elder-care assistance, employee assistance programs (including psychological and family counseling and programs to deal with alcohol and substance abuse), maternity and family leave policies, and work scheduling options, among others. Although many U.S. companies have taken steps toward helping employees balance family and work, a study released in July 1998 found many employers still lack even basic work/family policies.[21]

The "Business Work-Life Study" by the Families and Work Institute, one of the first comprehensive assessments of the availability of corporate work-family programs, reports that workers with more supportive employers were more likely to be loyal to their companies. The study noted the gaps between widespread corporate rhetoric given to work-family concerns and the actual help given to workers. Many firms don't make a real effort to let their workers know that help is available. They don't hold managers responsible for being sensitive to family needs. Even in companies with progressive family benefits package, many employees believe that taking advantage of the company's parental benefit programs would jeopardize their careers.

Nearly 90 percent of the 1,000 companies examined allow workers to take time off to attend school events, and half let workers stay home with mildly ill children without using vacations or sick days. Half the companies surveyed provide dependent-care assistance plans, allowing employees to set aside wages on a pre-tax basis for childcare or other dependent-care expenses. Of the companies surveyed, 33 percent offer maternity leaves more than 13 weeks long, and 23 percent offer elder care resource and referral services as part of their employee assistance program. Yet only nine percent of companies offer childcare at or near the workplace.

The "Business Work-Life Study" focused on companies that employ 100 workers or more, and found that two-thirds of these employers permit flex-time. That is, they allow employees to adjust their work hours on a daily basis.

The Stride Rite Corporation, a Cambridge, Massachusetts, shoe manufacturer was one of a handful of pioneers when it started a childcare center at its Roxbury plant in 1971. A few other progressive companies with a large proportion of female workers followed Stride Rite's lead in the early 1980s. These companies bucked the tide against what was then a politically sensitive issue and established maternity leave policies, but most companies at that time were not particularly receptive to the idea.[22]

One-size-fits-all employees and practices are outdated. The workplace has changed, and the people within it have changed, and employers need to acknowledge the reality. The kinds of skills managers need to manage the current work force are different in today's competitive economic environment. It is more than simply being nice to employees—it makes good business sense. Sufficient evidence exists that work and family initiatives have a tremendous pay-off for companies wise enough to invest in them. Employers in tight labor markets find that work and family benefits allow them to compete successfully for the best employees. Reduced turnover and absenteeism along with increased productivity are a few of the "employer benefits" that can be gained when companies truly are committed to helping employees balance work and family.

Woman-Owned Businesses

The rise of women's entrepreneurship has been called "one of the most significant and one of the quietest revolutions of our time." Women may be leaving corporate America, but they are not leaving the work force. Dun & Bradstreet reports that women-owned businesses are not only one of the most rapidly expanding sectors of the economy, but also a financially stable sector.[23]

- In 1999, there were 9.1 million woman-owned businesses in the United States, employing more than 27.5 million people and generating over $3.6 trillion in sales.

- The number of woman-owned businesses more than doubled between 1987 and 1999, employment tripled, and sales grew by 436 percent.

- More than one in five employees works for a woman-owned firm.

- Employment by woman-owned firms rose more than 100 percent from 1987 to 1992, compared with the national average of 38 percent.

- Employment in woman-owned firms with 100 or more workers increased by 158 percent, more than twice the rate for all U.S. companies of similar size.

- Growth in woman-owned businesses has been particularly strong in the construction, wholesale trade, transportation/communications, agribusiness, and manufacturing industries.

- Women-owned businesses are as financially sound and creditworthy as the typical firm in the U.S. economy, and are more likely to remain in business than the average U.S. firm.

- Nearly three-fourths of woman-owned companies in business in 1991 were still in business three years later, compared with two-thirds for all U.S. companies.

- As of 1992, 13 percent of woman-owned companies—about the same as the percentage for all U.S. businesses—were involved in international trade.

Women business owners agree that the greatest rewards are derived from being in charge of one's own fate. Women business owners cite the following reasons as the rewards of business ownership:

- Having control over their own destiny
- Satisfaction of building and growing a business
- Employing people and helping them achieve their full potential
- Gaining independence and freedom
- Achieving growth and personal balance
- The associated financial rewards
- Overcoming gender-related obstacles
- A feeling of pride and self-esteem.[24]

Looking Toward the Future

Women are no longer content to simply gain entry to the profession of their choice. They want to be part of the leadership and to be equally compensated for their contributions. They also want control over their lives and the freedom to not be penalized if they choose to have children. Hopefully achieving these goals will not be as difficult, nor as much of a battle, for the current generation of women as gaining entry to the professions was for past generations.

Most of the legislative framework is in place to facilitate our country's transition to a less sexist and less racist future. Remembering, however, that it took 72 years for women to get the right to vote once the battle began, it may be too much to ask for full equality across all facets of our working and personal lives now.

However, women are making tremendous strides toward that equality in the workplace and in those professions that have been traditionally the province of men. As women become accomplished and recognized in all fields of endeavor, equality edges ever closer.

Endnotes

Preface

1. Jackson, Maggie, "Women Start Own Firms in Frustration," The *Denver Post*, February 25, 1998, p. 3C.
2. Clinton, William J., A Proclamation by the President of the United States for Women's History Month 2000, March 2000.

Introduction

1. In the 17th century, between 25 and 50 percent of all women died in childbirth or from childhood diseases. The average life expectancy was 45. Taylor, Dale, *The Writer's Guide to Everyday Life in Colonial America From 1607-1783*, Cincinnati, Ohio: Writer's Digest Books, 1997, p. 129. The average life expectancy in 1900 was 48 years. Rosenfeld, Isadore, Dr., "Why We're Healthier Today," *Parade Magazine*, March 19, 2000, p. 4. The average male life expectancy in 2000 is 80.1 years and 84.3 for women. Clements, Jonathan, "The Many Ways to Play the Averages," The *Wall Street Journal*, March 28, 2000, p. C1.
2. This is a fictional scenario based on actual experiences of the authors.
3. Garza, Hedda, *Women in Medicine*, New York: Franklin Watts, 1994, p. 32. Harris, Barbara, *Beyond Her Sphere: Women in the*

Professions in American History, Westport, Connecticut: Greenwood Press, 1978, Chapter 2, The Cult of Domesticity. Stubblefield, Harold W. and Patrick Keane, *Adult Education in the American Experience: From the Colonial Period to the Present*, San Francisco: Jossey-Bass, 1994, pp. 152-153. Zinn, Howard, *A People's History of the United States: 1492-Present*, New York: Harper Perennial, 1995, pp. 111-113.

4. Stubblefield and Keane, op.cit., pp. 41-43. "Franklin, Benjamin," Funk & Wagnalls Multimedia Encyclopedia, http://versaware.refe . . .ook=FWENCOnline&page=009001352.asp, accessed November 27, 2000, p. 2.

5. Harris, op.cit., pp. 38-39. Zinn, op.cit., p. 109.

6. Farrell, Christopher, "Women in the Workplace: Is Parity Finally in Sight?" *Business Week*, August 9, 1999, p. 35.

Chapter One: Setting the Stage

1. Zinn, Howard, *A People's History of the United States:1492-Present*, New York: Harper Perennial, 1995, p. 102.

2. The "Old Country" as referred to in this volume for the colonial period is primarily European countries. In the late 1800s and early 1900s, the "Old Country" often came to mean Eastern Europe and includes Russia and the Commonwealth of Independent States. Garza, Hedda, *Women in Medicine*, New York; Franklin Watts, 1994, p. 23. Flexner, Eleanor and Ellen Fitzpatrick, *Century of Struggle: The Women's Rights Movement in the United States*, Enlarged Edition, Cambridge, Massachusetts: The Belknap Press of Harvard University Press, 1996, p. 3.

3. Flexner, Eleanor and Ellen Fitzpatrick, op.cit., pp. 5-6.

4. Ibid., p.7. Baer, Judith A., *Women in American Law: The Struggle Toward Equality From the New Deal to the Present*, 2nd Edition, New York: Homes & Meier, 1996, p. 15.

5. Baer, Judith A., op.cit., p 20. Flexner and Fitzpatrick, op.cit., p. 157. Zinn, op.cit., p. 109. Garza, Hedda, *Barred From the Bar: A*

History of Women in the Legal Profession, New York: Franklin Watts, 1996, p. 15.

6. Flexner and Fitzpatrick, op.cit., p. 8.

7. Ibid.

8. Because of the approach of most textbooks and historical documents, this history primarily captures what has been written by and about Caucasian Americans.

9. Flexner and Fitzpatrick, op.cit., pp. 9-11.

10. Zinn, op.cit., p. 108.

11. Flexner and Fitzpatrick, op. cit, p. 22.

12. Harris, Barbara, *Beyond Her Sphere: Women in the Professions in American History,* Westport, Connecticut: Greenwood Press, 1978, pp. 13-18. Dexter, Elizabeth Anthony, *Career Women of America: 1776-1840,* Francetown, New Hampshire: Marshall Jones Company, 1950, p.1. Chamberlain, Mariam K., Ed., *Women in Academe: Progress and Prospects,* New York: Russell Sage Foundation, 1988, p. 5. Rossiter, Margaret W., *Women Scientists in America: Struggles and Strategies to 1940,* Baltimore, Maryland: The Johns Hopkins University Press, 1982, pp. 13-14.

13. Baer, op. cit, pp. 221-222.

14. Harris, Barbara, op.cit., p. 18. Zinn, op.cit., p. 109.

15. Baer, op.cit., p. 221.

16. *Webster's Dictionary of American Women,* New York: SMITHMARK Publishers, 1996, pp. 648-649. Flexner and Fitzpatrick, op.cit., pp. 35-36.

17. Zinn, op.cit., pp. 88-90.

18. Zinn, op.cit., p. 109. Garza, 1996, op.cit., p. 15.

19. Flexner and Fitzpatrick, op.cit., p. 14. Zinn, op.cit., p. 109. Garza, 1996, op.cit., p. 17. "John Adams," http://gi.Grolier.com/presidents/ea/bios/02pjohn.html, accessed November 22, 2000, p. 1.

20. Baldwin, Louis, *Women of Strength: Bibliographies of 106 Who Have Excelled in Traditionally Male Fields, A.D. 61 to the Present,* Jefferson, North Carolina: McFarland & Company, 1996, p. 59.

21. Flexner and Fitzpatrick, op.cit. pp. 13-14. Zinn, op.cit., p.

109. Garza, 1996, op.cit., p. 19.

22. Flexner and Fitzpatrick, op.cit., p. 14. Zinn, op.cit., p. 109.

23. Baer, op.cit., 21.

24. Asby, Ruth and Ohrn, Deborah Gore, Eds., *Her Story: Women Who Changed the World*, New York: Viking Press, 1995, p. 71. Rossiter, Margaret, 1982, op.cit., p. 2. Flexner and Fitzpatrick, op.cit., p. 14.

25. Zinn, op. cit., p. 110.

26. Flexner and Fitzpatrick, op.cit. pp. 14-15. Baer, op.cit., p. 20. Garza, 1996, op.cit., p. 21.

27. Flexner and Fitzpatrick, op.cit., p. 16. Dexter, op.cit., p. 20. Rossiter, 1982, op.cit., p. 319. Stubblefield, Harold W. and Patrick Keane, *Adult Education in the American Experience: From the Colonial Period to the Present*, San Francisco: Jossey-Bass, 1994, p. 107.

28. Dexter, op.cit., pp. 25-27. Chamberlain, op.cit., p. 108.

29. Dexter, op.cit., pp.1-4.

30. Flexner and Fitzpatrick, op.cit., p. 22.

31. Dexter, op.cit., Chapter 1. This book contains an informative and light-hearted view of some of the more interesting "dames" of the colonial and New Republic eras.

32. Flexner and Fitzpatrick, op.cit., p. 22.

33. Stubblefield and Keane, op.cit., p. 108.

34. Flexner and Fitzpatrick, op.cit., p. 27. Harris, op.cit., p. 79.

35. Flexner and Fitzpatrick, op.cit., p. 28. Harris, op.cit., p. 79.

36. Harris, op.cit., pp. 79-80.

37. Ibid.

38. Flexner and Fitzpatrick, op.cit., p. 28.

39. Dexter, op.cit., pp. 7-9.

40. Ibid.

41. Sources for sections on minority education include Baer; Chamberlain; Flexner and Fitzpatrick; Garza, 1996; and Stubblefield and Keane.

42. Stubblefield and Keane, op.cit., p. 121.

43. Flexner and Fitzpatrick, op.cit., p. 35. Stubblefield and Keane,

op.cit., p. 128.
44. Stubblefield and Keane, op.cit., p. 125.
45. Ibid., p. 124-128.
46. Flexner and Fitzpatrick, op.cit., p. 23. Zinn, op.cit., p. 110.
47. Flexner and Fitzpatrick, op.cit., p. 23.
48. Zinn, op.cit. p. 110.
49. Ibid., p. 114.
50. Flexner and Fitzpatrick, op.cit., p. 223.
51. Ibid., pp. 249-254.
52. Zinn, op.cit., pp. 115-116. Flexner and Fitzpatrick, op.cit., p. 29.
53. Harris, op.cit., p.76. Zinn, op.cit., p. 116.
54. DuBois, Ellen, "Freedom: The Women's Rights Movement in a Word," *Living the Legacy*, National Women's History Project, 1998, p. 5.
55. In fact, this backlash has happened many times since the 1800s including in the 1970s when the Equal Rights Amendment failed to get enough states to ratify it and in the 1990s when the "Family Values" campaign was undertaken.
56. Zinn, op.cit., p. 113.
57. Harris, op.cit., p. 81.
58. Ibid., p. 84.
59. Ibid., pp. 84-85..
60. "Declaration of Sentiments," http://www.rochester.edu/SBA/declare.html, accessed March 9, 1999.
61. Ibid.
62. Flexner and Fitzpatrick, op.cit., p. 70 and p. 138.
63. "Emma Willard School," www.cr.nps.gov/nr/travel/pwwmh/ny17.htm, accessed March 14, 2000, p. 1. Brackett, Anna C., editor. *Woman and The Higher Education*. New York: Harper and Brothers, 1893, p. 2. Flexner and Fitzpatrick, op.cit., pp. 24-28. Rossiter, 1982, op.cit., pp. 4-6. "Emma Willard School," http://www.emma.troy.ny.us, accessed March 14, 2000. Garza, 1996, op.cit., pp. 62-63. Zinn, op.cit., pp. 116-117. *Webster's Dictionary of American Women*, New

York: SMITHMARK Publishers, 1996, pp. 661-662.

64. "Mary Lyon 1797-1849," www.greatwomen.org.lyon.htm, accessed July 27, 2000. Gilchrist, Beth Bradford, *The Life of Mary Lyon*, New York: Houghton Mifflin Company, 1910, p. 158. Mount Holyoke Female Seminary was opened on November 8, 1837. It became Mount Holyoke Seminary and College in 1888 and Mount Holyoke College in 1895. It remains one of the leading institutions for women in the U.S. Webster's, op.cit., p. 388. Flexner and Fitzpatrick, op.cit., pp. 32-35.

65. "Beecher, Catherine Esther (1800-1878), www.worldbook.com/fun/whm/html/whm090.html, accessed July 27, 2000. "Catherine Beecher, 'Domestic Economy," www.depaul.edu/~clio/CBeecher.htm, accessed July 31, 2000, p.1. Dexter, op.cit., pp. 23-25.

66. "Prudence Crandall 1803-1890," www.ctforum.org/cwhf/crandall.htm, accessed July 27, 2000. Foner, Philip S. and Josephine F. Pacheco, *Three Who Dared: Prudence Crandall, Margaret Douglass, Myrtilla Miner—Champions of Antebellum Black Education*, Westport, Connecticut: Greenwood Press, 1984, p.8. Flexner and Fitzpatrick, op.cit., pp. 36-37.

67. Zinn, p. 120. Webster, op.cit., p 252. Harris, pp. 81-84. Flexner and Fitzpatrick, op.cit., pp. 41-50. Garza, 1996, op.cit., pp. 27-28. Campbell, Karlyn Kohrs, Editor, *Women Public Speakers in the United States, 1800-1925: A Bio-Critical Sourcebook*, Westport, CT: Greenwood Press, 1993, pp. 206-207.

Chapter Two: Preparing to Fight

1. Harris, Barbara, *Beyond Her Sphere: Women in the Professions in American History*, Westport, Connecticut: Greenwood Press, 1978, pp. 75-79.

2. Ibid., p. 86. Flexner, Eleanor and Ellen Fitzpatrick, *Century of Struggle: The Women's Rights Movement in the United States*, Enlarged Edition, Cambridge, Massachusetts: The Belknap Press of Harvard

University Press, 1996, pp. 73-79.

3. Flexner and Fitzpatrick, op.cit., pp. 80-83 and p. 222. Garza, Hedda, *Barred From the Bar: A History of Women in the Legal Profession*, New York: Franklin Watts, 1996, p. 29.

4. Rossiter, Margaret, *Women Scientists in America: Struggles and Strategies to 1940*, Baltimore, Maryland: The Johns Hopkins University Press, 1982, p. 100. Margaret Rossiter contends that feminism, as a political doctrine, did not become a strong ideology among professional women until the 1910s. There is sufficient other evidence that suggests that professional women were fully involved in women's rights issues at a much earlier stage.

5. Harris, op.cit., p. 110.

6. Ibid, p. 104-105.

7. "Declaration of Sentiments, Seneca Falls, New York, 1848," http://www.closeup.org/sentiment.htm, accessed April 11, 2000. Harris, op.cit., p. 74.

8. "Amendments to the Constitution," http://www.law.emory/edu/FEDERAL/usconst/amend.html, accessed April 11, 2000.

9. Flexner and Fitzpatrick, op.cit., pp. 136-137.

10. Ibid., pp. 137-139.

11. Ibid., pp. 137-138.

12. Ibid., p. 141.

13. Ibid., p. 138.

14. Ibid, p. 138.

15. Ibid., pp. 138-139.

16. Rossiter, 1982, op.cit., p. 74.

17. Flexner and Fitzpatrick, op.cit., pp. 26-27.

18. Ibid., pp. 30-35. Harris, op.cit., pp. 79-80. *Webster's Dictionary of American Women*, New York: SMITHMARK Publishers, 1996, p. 388. Mount Holyoke would not become a college until 1888.

19. Harris, op.cit., p. 79. Flexner and Fitzpatrick, op.cit., p. 28.

20. Rossiter, 1982, op.cit., pp. 4-10. Flexner, op.cit., pp. 30-35 and pp. 116-121. Harris, op.cit., p. 79 and pp. 98-100. Smith College

was chartered in 1871 and opened in 1875 with 14 students. Webster, op.cit., p. 575.

21. Flexner and Fitzpatrick, op.cit., pp. 118-120.

22. Harris, op.cit., p. 98. The Morrill Act of 1862 signed into law by President Lincoln gave 10,000 acres of federal government land to each state to sell and use the proceeds to create a public university to teach agriculture and the mechanic (engineering) arts. The land grant universities today still have the major responsibility for agricultural research and teaching responsibility as well as a major "outreach" or extension education mission to the public. "The Land Grant System of Education in the United States," http://www.ag.ohio-state.edu/~ohioline/lines/lgrant.html, accessed April 11, 2000.

23. Harris, op.cit., p. 99.

24. Ibid., pp. 100-105.

25. Stubblefield, Harold W. and Patrick Keane, *Adult Education in the American Experience: From the Colonial Period to the Present*, San Francisco: Jossey-Bass, 1994, pp. 120, 121, and 123.

26. Flexner and Fitzpatrick, op.cit., p. 35.

27. Stubblefield and Keane, op.cit., pp. 125-131.

28. Harris, op.cit., pp. 104-15. Flexner and Fitzpatrick, op.cit., p. 108. This source states "According to one modern definition, "professions involve essentially intellectual operations with large individual responsibility; they derive their raw material from science and learning; this material they work up to a practical and definite end; they possess an educationally communicable technique; they tend to self-organization."

29. Rossiter, 1982, op.cit., pp. 28-29.

30. Ibid., p. 29.

31. Ibid., p. 30.

32. Ibid.

33. Ibid, pp. 30-31.

34. Ibid., p. 33-35.

35. Harris, op.cit., p. 145. Morello, Karen Berger, *The Invisible Bar: The Woman Lawyer in America: 1638 to the Present*, New York:

Notes 175

Random House, 1986, pp. 101-104. Lopez, Enrique Hank, *The Harvard Mystique: The Power Syndrome That Affects our Lives From Sesame Street to the White House*, New York: MacMillan Publishing Co., Inc., 1979, p. 55. Chamberlain, Mariam K., Ed., *Women in Academe: Progress and Prospects*, New York: Russell Sage Foundation, 1988, p. 359.

36. Rossiter, 1982, op.cit., pp. 73-99. See also Glazer, Penina Migdal and Miriam Slater, *Unequal Colleagues: The Entrance of Women Into the Professions, 1890 – 1940*, New Brunswick, NJ: Rutgers, University Press, 1987, p. 224.

37. Chamberlain, op.cit., pp. 109-110. Rossiter, 1982, op.cit., pp. 10-12.

38. Chamberlain, op.cit., pp. 111-112. "Tuskegee Institute: National Historic Site," http://www.nps.gov/tuin/, accessed April 19, 2000. Maxwell, Joe, "The Legacy of Booker T. Washington: A Family Reunion," November, 1996, http://www.capitalresearch.org/pcs/pcs-1196.html, accessed April 19, 2000, p. 1.

39. Chamberlain, op.cit., p.112.

40. Ibid.

41. Ibid. Flexner and Fitzpatrick, op.cit., p. 123.

42. Flexner and Fitzpatrick, op.cit., pp. 223-224. Harris, op.cit., pp. 87, and 106-107.

43. Harris, op.cit., pp. 110-112. Flexner and Fitzpatrick, op.cit., pp. 115-116 and 174. Morello, op.cit., pp. 108-113. Garza, 1996, op.cit., pp. 71-73.

44. Flexner and Fitzpatrick, op.cit., pp. 92-95. Webster, op.cit.,, pp. 426-427.

45. Rossiter, 1982, op.cit., pp. 30-31, 38-39, 68-70, and others. Kass-Simon, G., and Patricia Farnes, Editors, *Women of Science: Righting the Record*, Bloomington, Indiana: Indiana University Press, 1990, pp. 150-157.

46. Rossiter, 1982, op.cit., pp. 31, 38-46, 279-281. Webster, op.cit., p. 347.

47. Abrams, Ruth J. Ed., *Send Us a Lady Physician: Women*

Doctors in America, 1835-1920, New York: W.W. Northon & Company, 1985, Introduction. Garza, Hedda, *Women in Medicine,* New York: Franklin Watts, 1994, p. 39-40, 43-44, and 46-48. Harris, op.cit., p. 61, 88-90, and 105-108. Webster, op. cit., pp. 55-56. Flexner and Fitzpatrick, op.cit., pp. 223-224.

48. Garza, 1996, op.cit., p. 50. "III. The Gibbs Affair at Columbia College (1853-1854)," http:/beatl.barnard.columbia.edu/learn/GibbsAffair.htm, accessed August 29, 2000, p. 1.

49. Morello, op.cit., pp. 108-142. Morello profiles many of the pioneering women in law in her Chapter 5 – "Rebels and Reformers."

Chapter Three: Women Attempt to Reform Society

1. Zinn, Howard, *A People's History of the United States: 1492-Present,* New York: Harper Perennial, 1995, pp. 116, 118, and 123.

2. Flexner, Eleanor and Ellen Fitzpatrick, *Century of Struggle: The Women's Rights Movement in the United States,* Enlarged Edition, Cambridge, Massachusetts: The Belknap Press of Harvard University Press, 1996, p. 196 and 38.

3. Ibid., p. 76.

4. Zinn, op.cit., pp. 116, 118 and 123. Morello, Karen Berger, *The Invisible Bar: The Woman Lawyer in America: 1638 to the Present,* New York: Random House, 1986, p. 108. Flexner and Fitzpatrick, op.cit., pp. 38, 105, and 137. Garza, Hedda, *Barred From the Bar: A History of Women in the Legal Profession,* New York: Franklin Watts, 1996, p. 30.

5 "Amendments to the Constitution," http://www.law.emory/edu/FEDERAL/usconst/amend.html, accessed April 11, 2000.

6. Flexner and Fitzpatrick, op.cit., Preface, 1975, p. xxxiii.

7. Ibid., p. 157.

8. Ibid., pp. 286-287.

9. Garza, Hedda, *Women in Medicine,* New York: Franklin Watts, 1994, p. 66. From the 1880s to 1960s, a majority of American states

Notes 177

enforced segregation through "Jim Crow" laws (named after a black character in minstrel shows). From Delaware to California, and from North Dakota to Texas, many states (and cities) could impose legal punishments on people for consorting with members of another race. The most common types of laws forbade intermarriage and ordered business owners and public institutions to keep their black and white clientele separated. Here are the categories of some of the state laws: nurses, buses, railroads, restaurants, pool and billiard rooms, toilet facilities, intermarriage, education, juvenile delinquents, mental hospitals, barbers, burial, amateur baseball, parks, wine and beer, reform schools, circus tickets, housing, the blind, hospital entrances, prisons, textbooks, libraries, militia, transportation, teaching, mining, telephone booths, lunch counters, child custody, and theaters. "'Jim Crow' Laws," http://www.nps.gov/malu/documents/jim_crow_laws.htm, accessed April 20, 2000, p.1. Flexner and Fitzpatrick, op.cit., pp. 286-287.

10. Flexner and Fitzpatrick, op.cit., p. 295.
11. Ibid., pp. 73-74 and p. 89.
12. Ibid., pp. 88-89.
13. Ibid., pp. 297-298.
14. Ibid., p. 297-299.
15. Ibid., pp. 297-298.
16. Ibid., p. 297.
17. Ibid., p. 287.
18. Ibid., pp. 287-289.
19. Wheeler, Marjorie Spruill, "The History of the Suffrage Movement," http://www.pbs.org/onewoman/suffrage.html, accessed April 28, 1999, p. 4.
20. Flexner and Fitzpatrick, op.cit., pp. 288-289. Their fear of women's influence in pushing for Prohibition was theoretically well-founded, but, as it turned out, Prohibition was enacted in 1919, more than a year before the suffragist amendment was ratified. Garza, 1996, op.cit., p. 77.
21. Ibid., pp. 289-290.
22. Ibid., p. 290. Tammany Hall was formed shortly after the

American Revolution when some members of the Tammany Society formed a political wing named after the place where they met. Not until the middle of the nineteenth century, did Tammany come to be seen as a powerful, political machine. It existed until the early 1960s. Allen, Oliver E., *The Tiger: The Rise and Fall of Tammany Hall*, New York, NY: Addison-Wesley Publishing Company, 1993, pp. ix-xi.

23. Flexner and Fitzpatrick, op.cit., pp. 291-292.

24. Ibid., p. 293.

25. Ibid., pp. 139-143 and p. 165. Irwin, Inez Hayes, *The Story of Alice Paul and The National Woman's Party*, Fairfax, Virginia: Denlinger's Publishers, Ltd., 1977, p. 37.

26. Flexner and Fitzpatrick, op.cit., pp. 145-146.

27. Spruill, op.cit, p. 2, and Flexner and Fitzpatrick, op.cit., pp. 145-147.

28. Spruill, op.cit., p. 2, and Flexner and Fitzpatrick, op.cit., pp. 146 and 208.

29. Flexner and Fitzpatrick, op.cit., pp. 211-212.

30. Ibid., pp. 209-210.

31. Ibid., pp. 213-214. Garza, 1996, op.cit., pp. 70-72.

32. Flexner and Fitzpatrick, op.cit., pp. 214-217.

33. Ibid., pp. 215-216. "history: biographies, William Randolph Hearst," www.hearstcastle.org/hearstcastle.bio_wrhearst.html, accessed July 7, 2000. "History: The Founding of the University," www.Stanford.edu/home/Stanford/history/begin/html, accessed July 7, 2000.

34. Flexner and Fitzpatrick, op.cit., pp. 215-216.

35. Ibid., p. 221.

36. Ibid.

37. Ibid., pp. 221-222. Code Napoleon is the designation officially applied in 1807 to the code of French civil law originally enacted in March 1804 as the Code Civil des Francais and still in force in France. An initial draft was completed in 1793. The code is named in honor of Napoleon, emperor of France, who had participated in the formulation. The term applies to the entire body of French law as contained in five codes dealing with civil, commercial, and criminal law, promulgated

between 1804 and 1811. The code was introduced into a number of European countries, notably Belgium, where it is still in force. It was the model for the civil codes of Quebec Province, Canada, the Netherlands, Italy, Spain, some Latin American republics, and the state of Louisiana. As written, the Code Napolon has a number of weaknesses with regard to women and minors:

A. A woman could not vote.
B. A wife owed obedience to her husband, who had total control over their property.
C. An unmarried woman had few rights and could not be a legal guardian or witness wills.
D. It was easier for a man to sue for divorce on grounds of adultery, while a man had to cohabit with his mistress for two years for his wife to justify a divorce.
E. If a man surprised his wife in bed with another man, he could kill her legally. If a woman did so, she could be tried for murder.
F. Minors had few rights. A father could even place his child in jail for up to six months.
G. Illegitimate children had no rights of inheritance.

Burnham, Robert, "#8: The Code Napoleon," Frequently Asked Questions (FAQ), The Napoleon Series, www.historyserver.org/napoleon.series/faq/c_code.html, accessed July 10, 2000. "Code Napoleon," Microsoft ® Encarta ® Online Encyclopedia 2000, http://Encarta.msn.com © 1997-2000 Microsoft Corporation, accessed July 10, 2000.

    38. Flexner and Fitzpatrick, op.cit., p. 222.
    39. Ibid., p. 222.
    40. Ibid., pp. 241, 244-247, and 255.
    41. Ibid., pp. 229-232.
    42. *Webster's Dictionary of American Women*, New York: SMITHMARK Publishers, 1996, p. 100. "Miriam Leslie: Belle of the Boardroom," From *Smithsonian Magazine*, November 1997, http://www.smithsonianmag.si.edu/s. . .n/issues97/nov97/Miriam_nov97.html. Flexner and Fitzpatrick reference *The History of*

Women Suffrage in describing the bequest from Miriam Leslie. They further report on page 341 that *The History of Women's Suffrage* was published in six volumes. Volumes I to III were edited by Elizabeth Cady Stanton, Susan Anthony, and Mathilda Joslyn Gage. The first two volumes were published in Rochester, New York, in 1881; the third in 1886. Volume IV, edited by Susan B. Anthony and Ida Husted Harper, was published in Rochester in 1902. Volumes V and VI were edited by Ida Husted Harper and published in New York in 1922. Flexner and Fitzpatrick, op.cit., p. 265.

43. Blake, Kellee, "First in the Path of the Fireman: The Fate of the 1890 Population Census," www.nara.gov/publications/prologue/1890cen1.html, accessed August 23, 2000, p. 2. "NPG Facts and Figures: Historical U.S. Population Growth by year 1900-1998," www.npg.org/facts/us_historical_pops.htm, accessed August 23, 2000, p. 3.

44. Flexner and Fitzpatrick, op.cit., pp. 222-223.

45. Ibid., pp. 280-281.

46. Ibid, p. 280.

47. Ibid., p. 280. Concerns such as working unlimited hours and working conditions led to the creation of special agencies to address the issues. The establishment of the Women's Bureau of the Department of Labor goes back initially to the needs of women workers in munition and ordnance plants, which led to setting up the Women's Division of the Ordnance Department, and subsequently to the establishment in June 1918 of the Women in Industry Service of the Department of Labor. The first director of the Women's Bureau was Mary Anderson, who assumed that position in 1920.

48. Ibid., p. 281.

49. Ibid.

50. Ibid., pp. 282-283.

51. Ibid., pp. 271-272 and p. 302.

52. Ibid., pp. 283-284.

53. Ibid, pp. 283. http://bioguide.congress.gov/biosearch/biosearch1.asp, accessed July 21, 2000.

54. Flexner and Fitzpatrick, op.cit., pp. 284-285. Both the Republican Party and the Democratic party at the time of the passage of the Nineteenth Amendment were different in structure and approach than the similarly-named parties in 2000. The Republican party was founded in 1854. The early Republicans were united in their opposition to extending slavery into the western territories. Abraham Lincoln was the Republican presidential candidate in 1860. From its beginnings, the party represented a nationalistic, Protestant, Anglo-Saxon American, committed to a strong federal government. In the late nineteenth century, the party increasingly emphasized the promotion of industrial values, and often had an anti-immigrant stance as well. Beginning in the 1890s, a group of Republicans known as the progressives sought to balance the party's commitment to the industrial elite with the use of federal power to correct some of the worst excesses of the monopolies and trusts that dominated the economy. The party has continued to evolve through the Great Depression, and the New Deal, World War II, and today, the dominance of conservatism. ["Republican Party, http://Encarta.msn.com/find/Concise.asp?ti-04241000, accessed July 11, 2000.]

The Democratic Party traces its origins to the coalition formed behind Thomas Jefferson in the 1790s to resist the policies of the George Washington administration. This coalition was originally called the Republican and later the Democratic-Republican Party. In the 1830s, the Democratic Party developed the characteristics it retained until the end of the century—use of national power in foreign affairs when America's interests are threatened, but in economic and social policy, the responsibility of the government to act cautiously, if at all. The party further believed that federal government should not do anything the states could do for themselves, and that the states should not do what localities could do. By the late 1800s, the party was split into three factions that were not united until after the Great Depression. These three factions had positions as follows: 1) conventional policies of limited government, 2) urban political machines with strong immigrant support, and 3) angry farmers and small-town entrepreneurs who wanted more vigorous government intervention on their behalf. [Democratic Party, http://Encarta.msn.com/find/Concise.asp?ti=02777000, accessed July 11, 2000]

55. Baer, Judith A., *Women in American Law: The Struggle Toward Equality From the New Deal to the Present*, 2nd Edition, New York: Homes & Meier, 1996, p. 55. Amendment process: Article V of the constitution establishes several amending processes, only one of which has been used with any frequency. An amendment may be proposed by a two-thirds vote of both houses of Congress and ratified by three-fourths of the sate legislatures (it takes both houses, except in unicameral Nebraska to ratify). Congress may or may not, as it chooses, establish a time limit for ratification. "Winning the Right to Vote," www.greatwomen.org/lcvt.htm, accessed July 11, 2000. "The Nineteenth Amendment and the War of the Roses in Nashville," wysiwyg://16http://www.blueshoenashville.com/suffragehistory.html, accessed July 11, 2000, p. 2. Flexner and Fitzpatrick, op.cit., p. 232.

56. Flexner and Fitzpatrick, op.cit., p. 317.

57. Cromwell, Otelia, *Lucretia Mott*, Cambridge, Massachusetts: Harvard University Press, 1958, p. 150. Flexner and Fitzpatrick, op.cit, pp. 66-67 and 210. Webster, op.cit., pp. 443-444. "Lucretia Mott 1793-1880,: www.greatwomen.org/mott.htm, accessed July 11, 2000.

58. Flexner and Fitzpatrick, op.cit., pp. 84-86. Webster, op.cit., p. 621. "Sojourner Truth c.1797-1883," www.greatwomen.org/truth.htm, accessed July 11, 2000.

59. Flexner and Fitzpatrick, op.cit., pp. 67-71. Webster, op.cit., pp. 579-580. "Elizabeth Cady Stanton 1815-1902," www.greatwomen.org/stanton.htm, accessed July 11, 2000.

60. Flexner and Fitzpatrick, op.cit., pp. 59, 63-65, and 69-70. Webster, op.cit., pp. 589-590. Harris, Barbara, *Beyond Her Sphere: Women in the Professions in American History*, Westport, Connecticut: Greenwood Press, 1978, p. 87. "Lucy Stone 1818-1893," www.greatwomen.org/stone.htm, accessed July 11, 2000.

61. Flexner and Fitzpatrick, op.cit., pp. 79-84. Webster, op.cit.,

pp. 19-20. "Susan Brownell Anthony 1820-1906," www.greatwomen.org/anthony.htm, accessed July 11, 2000.
  62. Flexner and Fitzpatrick, op.cit., pp. 181-195. "Josephine St. Pierre Ruffin 1842-1924," www.greatwomen.org/ruffin.htm, accessed July 11, 2000.
  63. Webster, op.cit., pp. 564-565. "Anna Howard Shaw," ww.multimag.com/state/mi/womenshistory/ahshaw/, accessed July 11, 2000. "Anna Howard Shaw," www.multimag.com/state/mi/womenshistroy/ahshaw/bio.html, accessed July 31, 2000.
  64. Flexner and Fitzpatrick, op.cit., pp. 229-231. Webster, op.cit., pp. 100-101. "About Carrie Chapman Catt," www.catt.org/ccabout.html, accessed July 10, 2000. Harris, op. cit., p. 130.
  65. "Ida Bell Wells-Barnett 1862-1931," www.goddesscafe.com/FEMJOUR/wells.html, accessed July 11, 2000. Flexner and Fitzpatrick, op.cit., pp. 180-181, 298-299. "Ida Wells-Barnett 1862-1931," www.greatwomen.org/wbrnett.htm, accessed July 11, 2000. Garza, 1996, op.cit., p. 68.
  66. Hine, Darlene Clark, editor, *Black Women in United States History: Quest For Equality, The Life and Writings of Mary Eliza Church Terrell 1863-1954*, New York: Carlson Publishing, Inc., 1990, p. 63. "Legacy of Women Subject to Tuskegee University Research With Support of State Humanities Grant," www.tusk.edu/news_into/new/women.htm, accessed April 19, 2000. Webster, op.cit., pp. 607-609. Flexner and Fitzpatrick, op.cit., pp. 183-184.
  67. Flexner and Fitzpatrick, op.cit., pp. 255-257. Webster, op.cit., p. 478. "Alice Paul 1885-1977," www.greatwomen.org/paul.htm, accessed July 11, 2000. Irwin, op.cit., foreword and p. 76.

Chapter Four: Gaining a Foothold

  1. Harris, Barbara, *Beyond Her Sphere: Women in the Professions in American History*, Westport, Connecticut: Greenwood Press, 1978,

p. 128.

2. "Bridging Two Eras: The Autobiography of Emily Newell Blair, 1877-1951," Edited with an Introduction by Virginia Jeans Laas, http://system.missouri.edu/upress/fall1999/laas.htm, accessed July 18, 2000. "Heritage and Mission: Women's National Democratic Club," www.democraticwoman.org/heritage/, accessed July 18, 2000. Emily Newell Blair lived from 1877-1951 and believed that her life spanned two eras and that she was a bridge builder—able to reconcile a productive public life with the traditional values of housewife and mother. She became vice chairman of the Democratic National Committee only two years after women gained the right to vote. In 1922, Blair, then serving as the Democratic National Committee's vice chair and in charge of women's affairs, was the principal founder of the Woman's National Democratic Club. As the DNC official, Blair oversaw the organization of more than a thousand clubs for Democratic women throughout the country.

3. Harris, op.cit., pp. 127-128.

4. Ibid., p. 128.

5. Flexner, Eleanor and Ellen Fitzpatrick, *Century of Struggle: The Women's Rights Movement in the United States*, Enlarged Edition, Cambridge, Massachusetts: The Belknap Press of Harvard University Press, 1996, pp. 318-319. Harris, op.cit., pp. 130-131.

6. "Julia Clifford Lathrop," Microsoft ® Encarta ® 96 Encyclopedia. © 1993-1995 Microsoft Corporation, © Funk & Wagnalls Corporation, www.netsrq.com/~dboise/lathrop.html, accessed July 18, 2000. Flexner and Fitzpatrick, op.cit., p. 318.

7. Harris, op.cit., pp. 128-132.

8. Ibid., p. 137.

9. Chamberlain, Mariam K., Ed., *Women in Academe: Progress and Prospects*, New York: Russell Sage Foundation, 1988, p. 113.

10. Baer, Judith A., *Women in American Law: The Struggle Toward Equality From the New Deal to the Present*, 2nd Edition, New York: Homes & Meier, 1996, pp. 223-224. Seller, Maxine Schwartz, Ed., *Women Educators in the United States, 1820-1993*, Westport,

Connecticut: Greenwood Press, 1994, p. xxi. Harris, op.cit., pp. 117-118.

11. Baer, op.cit., pp. 224-228. Morello, Karen Berger, *The Invisible Bar: The Woman Lawyer in America: 1638 to the Present*, New York: Random House, 1986, pp. 88-90 and pp. 100-105.

12. Harris, op.cit., p. 141.

13. Seller, op.cit., pp. xxi - xxiii. "Butler, Mother Marie Joseph," Encyclopaedia Brittanica, www.brittanica.com/seo/m/mother-marie-joseph-butler/, accessed July 18, 2000. "Information for High School Students," www.saintmarys.edu/!incandel/highschool.html, accessed July 18, 2000.

14. "Alpha Kappa Alpha: History – The Founders," www.aka1908.com/slowe.htm, accessed July 18, 2000, p. 2. "Women Builders – Nannie Helen Burroughs," nttp://nmaa-tyder.si.edu/Johnson/burrough.html, accessed July 18, 2000. "People & Events: Nannie Helen Burroughs," www.pbs.org/wg...1900/peopleevents/pandeAMEX43.html, accessed July 18, 2000. "Mary McLeod Bethune 1875-1955," www.greatwomen.org, accessed July 18, 2000. "Mary McLeod Bethune Legacy Continuation Foundation, Inc.," http://users.erols.com/trirose/Bethune/Bethune.htm, accessed July 18, 2000.

15. Harris, op.cit, pp. 137-138. There was a five percent quota on female admissions to medical schools from 1925 to 1945. See also Garza, Hedda, *Women in Medicine*, New York: Franklin Watts, 1994, pp. 51-75.

16. Harris, op.cit., p. 138.

17. Ibid, p. 139.

18. Ibid.

19. Ibid., p. 152. Rossiter, Margaret W., *Women Scientists in America: Before Affirmative Action 1940-1972*, Baltimore, Maryland: The Johns Hopkins University Press, 1995, pp. 82-83. Ruth E. Moore earned the first doctorate of any black woman in bacteriology from Ohio State Univesity in 1933. Roger Arliner Young earned a doctorate in zoology from the University of Pennsylvania in 1940. She was fol-

lowed by Mary Logan Reddick and neuroembrologist Geraldine Pittman Woods at Radcliffe in 1944 and 1945, respectively. Marie Maynard Daly earned her doctorate in chemistry from Columbia in 1948, and Evelyn Boyd Granville her Ph.D. in mathematics from Yale in 1949. Marjorie Browne became the second black woman doctorate in mathematics at the University of Michigan in 1950.

20. Senate Reports, 78th Congress, 1st Session, January 6-December 21, 1943, Volume 2, Calendar No. 372, Report 363. "War Jobs for Women", Office of War Information, Magazine Section, Washington, DC, undated, pp. 19-20. Congressional Record, Proceedings and Debates of the 78th Congress, First Session, Index, Volume 89-Part 13, January 6, 1943 to December 21, 1943, Senate Bills 1100-1135, p. 662. Congressional Record, Proceedings and Debates of the 78th Congress, First Session, Volume 89 – Part 5, June 15, 1943, to July 6, 1943 (Pages 5839 to 7312). Harris, op.cit., pp. 152-153. "A Curriculum of United States labor History for Teachers, sponsored by the Illinois Labor History Society, www.kentlaw.edu/his/curricul.htm, accessed July 20, 2000, p. 19. "WLB: What It Is . . . How It Operates," A-2381, published by the National War Labor Board, undated, p. 7. The publication states under its responsibility for wage stabilization, "The following adjustments may, also, under certain conditions, be made without Board approval: increases to equalize rates paid to women for work of the same quantity and quality as work done by men in the same plant. . ."

21. Harris, op.cit., p. 153.

22. The Serviceman's Readjustment Act of 1944, often referred to as the GI Bill of Rights or GI Bill, helped approximately 2.25 million war veterans attend college. It was intended to smooth demobilization for America's almost 16 million servicemen and women. In addition to education benefits, millions of other GIs received job training; home, business, and farm loans; and unemployment benefits. "1940s: GI Bill," www.stampsonline.com/century/40bill.htm, accessed July 20, 2000. "Picture of the Day," February 28, The GI Bill, www.britishheritage.com/picture/0228.htm, accessed August 30, 2000. Baer, op.cit.,

p. 223. Seller, op.cit., p. xxii.
  23. Harris, op.cit., pp. 155-156.
  24. Ibid., p. 156 and p. 145.
  25. Ibid., pp. 156-157.
  26. Ibid., pp. 131-132, p. 148, p. 157. Like earlier splits in the suffragette movement, many social reformers continued to fight for state and federal legislation to protect women and children, as particularly vulnerable groups, from the worst forms of economic exploitation. Such protective legislation would be in areas such as laws prohibiting child labor, regulating the hours the females could work, setting minimum wages for women, and regulating labor conditions. Many women first joined the suffrage movement when their activities as social reformers had convinced them that the women needed the vote in order to achieve these types of legislative goals at both the state and federal levels.
  27. Harris, op.cit., p. 165.
  28. Ibid.
  29. Ibid., pp. 165-166.
  30. Ibid., p. 166. "Betty Friedan," www.gale.com/freresrc/womenhst/friedan.htm, accessed July 20, 2000, p. 1.
  31. Harris, op.cit., p. 168. "Gloria Steinem," www.goddesscafe.com/FEMJOUR/steinem.html, accessed July 20, 2000.
  32. Harris, op.cit., p. 167., Flexner and Fitzpatrick, p. 320.
  33. Harris, op.cit., p. 167.
  34. Ibid.
  35. Read, Phyllis J. and Bernard L. Witlieb, *The Book of Women's Firsts*, New York: Random House, 1992, pp. 342-343 and p. 419. Harris, op.cit., pp. 174-175. The Department of Labor was established by the U.S. Congress (Public Law 426-62: An Act to create a Department of Labor) in 1913. The Women's Bureau of the Department of Labor goes back initially to the needs of women workers in munitions and ordnance plants, which led to the formation of the Women's Division of the Ordnance Department, and subsequently to

the establishment in June 1918 of the Women in Industry Service of the Department of Labor. The Women's Bureau was established in 1920 and Mary Anderson served as its first director. Flexner and Fitzpatrick, op.cit., pp. 280-281. "The Organic Act of the Department of Labor," www.dol.gov/dol/asp/public/programs/history/organact.htm, accessed July 20, 2000, p. 1.

36. Read and Witlieb, op.cit., p. 419. Edith Green (1910 – 1987) served as a U.S. Representative from Oregon from 1955-1974. She is reported to have left a substantial legacy in the U.S. Congress. She left her mark on almost every education bill enacted during her tenure. Green supported federal aid to education and the anti-poverty programs of the Great Society while resisting expansion of the federal bureaucracy. She was appointed to the Committee on Education and Labor in her freshman term in the House of Representatives where she served until her final term in the House when she took a seat on the Committee on Appropriations. She served various terms on other House committees including Interior and Insular Affairs, House Administration, Merchant Marine and Fisheries, and District of Columbia. She authored the Higher Education Facilities Act of 1963 and the Higher Education Act of 1965. As chair of the Education and Labor subcommittee on higher education, she was responsible for establishing the first federal program for undergraduate scholarships. "Edith Starrett Green," www.clerkweb.house/gov/womenbio/Extended Bio/Green_edexb.htm, accessed July 20, 2000, p. 1. Harris, op.cit., p. 175. U.S. Department of Labor, Employment Standards Administration, Women's Bureau, *The Earnings Gap Between Women and Men*, 1976, p.6.

37. "Equal Pay Act of 1963," www.dot.gov/ost/docr/EQUALPAY.HTM, accessed July 21, 2000. Baer, op.cit., pp. 70-71.

38. Gallagher, Sean, "Federal Act prohibits unequal pay for equal work," The *Rocky Mountain News*, July 20, 1997, pp. 1J – 2J. D'Cruz, R. Jason, "Fair Labor Standards Act of 1938," www.mmmlaw.com/Articles/FairLaborStandardsAct of 1983.htm,

accessed August 23, 2000, p. 8.

39. Harris, op.cit., p. 175.

40. Baer, op.cit., p. 80. Harris, op.cit., p. 175.

41. Garza, Hedda, *Barred From the Bar: A History of Women in the Legal Profession*, New York: Franklin Watts, 1996, p. 117. Congresswoman Martha Griffiths, debating the inclusion of an amendment outlawing sex discrimination in Title VII of the Civil Rights Act of 1964.

42. Ibid. From a *New York Times* editorial ridiculing the inclusion of sex discrimination in Title VII.

43. Baer, op.cit., p. 80. Harris, op.cit., p. 175.

44. Harris, op.cit., p. 176. Affirmative action plans, however, have always been controversial—and never more so than in 1994, when the Republican Party sought and gained the support of "angry, white males." Baer, op.cit., p. 102.

45. Harris, op.cit., p. 176.

46. Ibid., pp. 176-177.

47. Flexner and Fitzpatrick, op.cit., pp. 321-322. Baer, p. 56. Irwin, Inez Hayes, *The Story of Alice Paul and The National Woman's Party*, Fairfax, Virginia: Denlinger's Publishers, Ltd., 1977, foreword. Alice Paul wrote the Equal Rights Amendment and under her leadership, the National Woman's Party had it introduced in Congress in 1923 and for 49 years thereafter. The original version, called the Lucretia Mott Amendment, read "Men and women shall have equal rights throughout the United States and in every place subject to its jurisdiction." Alice Paul consented to the revised wording of the amendment in 1943.

48. Baer, op.cit., p. 56. The National Consumers League was formed in 1899 to protect and promote the economic and social interests of America's consumers, using education, research, science, investigation, publications, and the public and private sector to accomplish that mission. The organization's priority is to promote the welfare of those consumers, wage earners, and income recipients least able to protect themselves, and to assist them in developing their own capabili-

ties to the extent possible. The League's promotion of a minimum wage led to the Fair Labor Standards Act of 1938. "Who We Are," www.natlconsumersleague.org/whoweare.htm, accessed July 21, 2000.

49. Baer, op.cit., p. 57.

50. Flexner and Fitzpatrick, p. 321-322. The amendment was introduced at each session of Congress even though it did not have political support and would not have any chance of being enacted during the Congressional session. Harris, op.cit., p. 176. Baer, op.cit., p. 55 and 58. Article V of the U.S. Constitution describes the amending process. Congress may or may not, as it chooses, establish a time limit for ratification. In the case of the ERA, the Congress later extended the deadline for ratification.

51. Baer, op. cit., p. 58.

52. Ibid., pp. 55-62.

53. Ibid., p. 60.

54. Ibid., pp.56 and 61-62

55. Webster, op.cit., p. 51. "Mary McLeod Bethune 1875-1955," www.greatwomen.org, accessed July 18, 2000. "Mary McLeod Bethune Legacy Continuation Foundation, Inc.," http://users.erols.com/trirose/Bethune/Bethune.htm, accessed July 18, 2000. "Profiles in Caring: Mary McLeod Bethune 1875-1955," www.nahc.org/NAHC/Val/Columns/SC10-6.html, accessed August 1, 2000, p. 1.

56. Read and Witlieb, op.cit., pp. 342-343. "President, First Lady Saddened At Death of Esther Peterson," News Release, December 23, 1997. "Esther Peterson 1906-1997," www.greatwomen.org/ptrson.htm, accessed July 21, 2000. "Peterson, Esther," Encyclopaedia Brittanica, www.brittanica.com/seo/e/esther-peterson/, accessed July 21, 2000. "Director's Gallery," www.dol.gov/dol/wb/gallery.htm, accessed July 20, 2000, p. 6.

57. "Betty Friedan," www.gale.com/freresrc/womenhst/friedan.htm, accessed July 20, 2000. Read and Witlieb, op.cit., p. 168. Webster, op.cit., pp. 214-215. "Betty Friedan 1921 – ", www.greatwomen.org/frdan.htm, accessed July

20, 2000.

58. Webster, op.cit., pp. 582-583. "Gloria Steinem 1934 - ," www.greatwomen.org/stnem.htm, accessed July 20, 2000. "Gloria Steinem b.1934," www.goddesscafe.com/FEMJOUR/steinem.html, accessed July 20, 2000. "Steinem, Gloria," an Encarta Encyclopedia article, http://Encarta.msn.com/index/conciseindex/1F/01F59000.htm?z=1@pg=2&br=1, accessed July 20, 2000. "Steinem, Gloria," Women in American History by Encyclopaedia Britannica, www.women.eb.com/women/articles/Steinem_Gloria.html, accessed November 27, 2000.

Chapter 5: Making Progress

1. Tobias, Sheila, *Faces of Feminism: An Activist's Reflections on the Women's Movement*, Boulder, CO: Westview Press, 1997, p. 104.
2. Ibid., pp. 104-105. More, Ellen S., *Restoring the Balance: Women Physicians and the Profession of Medicine, 1850-1995*, Cambridge, Massachusetts: Harvard University Press, 1999, p. 217.
3. Rossiter, Margaret W., *Women Scientists in America: Before Affirmative Action 1940-1972*, Baltimore, Maryland: The Johns Hopkins University Press, 1995, p. 382.
4. Baer, Judith A., *Women in American Law: The Struggle Toward Equality From the New Deal to the Present*, 2nd Edition, New York: Homes & Meier, 1996, p. 233. More, op.cit., pp. 217-218. "EEO/AA/Nondiscrimination Law & Policy for SDSU & CSU Institutions," www.sci.sdsu.edu/ODE/EEO_AA.html, accessed August 14, 2000, p. 1.
5. Tobias, op.cit., p. 122. Harris, Barbara, *Beyond Her Sphere: Women in the Professions in American History*, Westport, Connecticut: Greenwood Press, 1978, p. 183. Baer, op.cit., p. 233.
6. Tobias, op.cit., p. 123.
7. Harris, op.cit., p. 183.
8. Tobias, op.cit., p. 123.

9. Baer, op.cit., p. 233.

10. Harris, op.cit., p. 183. Tobias, op.cit., p. 123. Baer, op.cit., p. 234-237.

11. "Title IX of the Education Amendments of 1972 prohibits Discrimination Based on Sex in Education Programs or Activities which Receive Federal Financial Assistance," www.ed.gov/offices/OCR/tix_dis.html, accessed August 23, 2000, p 2.

12. Schroeder, Pat, *24 Years of House Work . . . and the Place is Still as Mess*, Kansas City: Andrews McMeel, 1998, pp. 197-198.

13. Tobias, op.cit., pp. 106-108.

14. Baer, op.cit., p. 81, Harris, op.cit., p. 183.

15. Tobias, op.cit., p. 115. The EEOC guidelines read: "Unwelcome sexual advances, requests for sexual favors, and other verbal or physical conduct of a sexual nature constitutes sexual harassment when (1) submission to such conduct is made either explicitly or implicitly a term or condition of an individual's employment or academic advancement, (2) submission to or rejection of such conduct...is used as the basis for employment decisions...or (3) such conduct has the purpose or effect of unreasonably interfering with an individual's work or academic performance or creating an intimidating hostile or offensive working or academic environment."

16. Ibid., pp. 115-117. Hill claimed to have endured continuing sexual invitations, innuendos, and intimation from Thomas during the 23 months that she worked for him. Although she had remained silent for almost 10 years, when his nomination for the Supreme Court was announced, she wrote an unsolicited negative evaluation to the Senate Judiciary Committee. This letter contained allegations in some detail of sexual harassment. When the committee delayed in responding to Hill's allegations, the letter was leaked to the press. A televised hearing was held and many Americans received a significant education about sexual harassment. Anita Hill had not brought charges against Clarence Thomas, fearful that she might be perceived to have solicited such advances, and believing that the issue would be perceived to be his word against hers.

17. "Coughlin v. Tailhook Association," www.lalabor.com/cases/shsa/tailhook1.html, accessed August 1, 2000, p. 2. "Tailhook Incident," www.now.org/issues/military/policies/tailhk.html, accessed August 1, 2000.

18. Tobias, op.cit., p. 125.

19. Ibid., pp. 125-126 Grove City College prides itself on its independence and does not accept federal aid of any kind. The Supreme Court case that limited the reach of Federal agency nondiscrimination requirements is known as *Grove City College v. T.H. Bell, Secretary U.S. Department of Education* 465 U.S. 555 (1984). "History and Mission," www.gcc.edu/history/main.asp, accessed August 1, 2000, p. 1. "Notice: Impacts of the Civil Rights Restoration Act of 1987 on FHWA Programs, www.fhwa.dot.gov/legsregs/directives/notices/n4720-6.htm, accessed August 1, 2000, p. 1. "Summary of Federal Laws," http://counsel.cua.edu/fedlaw/CR1987.htm, accessed August 1, 2000, p. 1. Baer, op.cit., p. 239.

20. "Geraldine Ferraro 1935 - ," www.greatwomen.org.frraro.htm, accessed August 1, 2000. "Rankin, Jeannette, 1880-1973," http://bioguide.congress.gov/scripts/biodisplay.pl?index=R000055, accessed August 1, 2000. "Women in Congress: Congresswomen's Biographies," http://bioguide.congress.gov/congresswomen/index.asp, accessed August 1, 2000. "Senate Statistics: Women in the Senate," www.senate.gov/learning/stat_14.html, accessed August 1, 2000, p. 1. Tanner, Robert, "Number of women in state office slips," Denver Rocky Mountain News, November 25, 2000, pp. 62A - 63A.

21. *Webster's Dictionary of American Women*, New York: SMITHMARK Publishers, 1996, pp. 462-463 and 234-235.

22. Seller, Maxine Schwartz, Ed., *Women Educators in the United States, 1820-1993*, Westport, Connecticut: Greenwood Press, 1994, p. xxiii.

23. "Brown v. Board of Education of Topeka," Kansas, www.infoplease.com/ce5/CE007737.html, accessed July 14, 1999. *Plessy v. Ferguson*, a case decided by the Supreme Court in 1896, upheld Louisiana's right to segregate railway carriages. The case concerned a

30-year-old African-American shoemaker named Homer Plessy who was jailed for sitting in the "white's" car of the East Louisiana Railroad. In what has been termed a "low" point for the judiciary, the Supreme Court determined that the fourteenth Amendment mandated political but not social equality. This ruling led to comprehensive Southern segregation laws that lasted for more than 50 years. "The African American Journey: Plessy v. Ferguson," www.worldbook.com/fun/aajourny/html/bh058.html, accessed November 29, 2000. "Plessy v. Ferguson," www.encyclopedia.com/articles/10297.html, accessed November 29, 2000. "Plessy v. Ferguson 1892," http://campus.northpark.edu/history//WebChron/USA/PlessyFerguson.html, accessed November 29, 2000, p. 1. *Plessy v. Ferguson,*" www.auaa.org/library/lb_ples.html, accessed November 29, 2000.

24. "Brown v. Board of Education," www.Watson.org/~lisa/blackhistory/early-civilrights/brown.html, accessed August 14, 2000, p. 2.

25. "History of Bilingual Education," *Rethinking Schools*, Volume 12, Number 3, Spring 1998, www.rethinkingschools.org/Archives/12_03/langhst.htm, accessed August 15, 2000, p. 1. "What court rulings have impacted the education of language minority students in the U.S.?," www.ncbe.gwu.edu/askncbe/faqs/07court.htm, accessed August 15, 2000. "U.S. Supreme Court – Law v. Nichols, 414 U.S. 563 (1974)," http://caselaw.findlaw...rt=US&navby=case&vol=414&invol=563, accessed August 15, 2000.

26. Seller, op.cit., pp. xxiii-xxiv. Examples of minority women who made significant contributions to the advancement of education include: African-American Septima Clark, who worked with the Southern Christian Leadership Council to teach disfranchised adults a curriculum of literacy specifically directed toward their political empowerment. Yakima educator Martha Yallup and Crow educator Janine Pease-Windy Boy developed colleges that prepared Native Americans to live successfully in "mainstream" America without abandoning their rich heritage. Mexican-American Dolores Gonzales, a pioneer in bilingual education, and a productive and respected scholar and administrator adopted an educational goal of preserving her people's language

and culture. Sucheng Chan, was instrumental in establishing the legitimacy of Asian studies on University campuses. Anthropologist Johnetta Cole played a unique role as president of Spelman College.

27. Chamberlain, Mariam K., Ed., *Women in Academe: Progress and Prospects*, New York: Russell Sage Foundation, 1988, p. 363. Barbett, Samuel F. and Roslyn A. Korb, U.S. Department of Education, National Center for Education Statistics, Enrollment in Higher Education: Fall 1995, July 1997, NCES 97-440, p. 7.

28. Chamberlain, op.cit., p. 40-43.

29. Harris, op.cit., p. 187.

30. *Engineers*, Engineering Workforce Commission, January 1998, p.12. Harris, op.cit., p. 187.

31. Chamberlain, op.cit., pp. 213, 239, and 241.

32. Rossi, Alice S. and Ann Calderwood, *Academic Women on the Move*, New York: Russell Sage Foundation, 1973. For a detailed discussion of the history and social implications of women's studies, see Chapter Seventeen. Chamberlain, op.cit., pp. 133-161, Chapter 7, "Women's Studies and Curricular Change."

33. Stubblefield, Harold W. and Keane, Patrick, *Adult Education in the American Experience: From the Colonial Period to the Present*, San Francisco: Jossey-Bass, 1994, p. 256.

34. Ibid.

35. Koerner, Brendan I., "Where the Boys Aren't," *U.S. News & World Report*, February 8, 1999, pp. 46-55.

36. Ibid, p. 47.

37. Ibid., p. 49.

38. "Education Pays!" http://titan.iwu.edu/~jplath/booster.html. Quoting from a Knight-Ridder/Tribune Service article from May 26, 1997.

39. Koretz, Gene, "Growing Gender Gap on Campus: Women's lead in enrollment is up," *Business Week*, February 15, 1999, p. 26.

40. Silver, Sheryl, "Author Says Technical Skills Not Always a Must," *Los Angeles Times*, July 25, 1999, www.latimes.com/class/employ/silver/silv990725.htm, accessed August

31, 2000, p. 1. Uhland, Vicky, "Hospitality Managers Cash in," *Denver Rocky Mountain News*, April 4, 1999, pp. J1-2.

    41. Koerner, op.cit., p. 48.

    42. Harris, op.cit., p. 184.

    43. "Excuse me, are women equal yet?" *Glamour*, February 1996, p. 91. The authors find it ironic that this type of editorial was found in a magazine with the name "Glamour." Representative Connie Morella (R-Md.) was quoted in the Glamour article as saying, "Without affirmative action, women as well as minorities would never have gotten as far as we have. Look at Eileen Collins, the first woman to pilot a space shuttle. If it weren't for affirmative action they would still be sending monkeys into space, but not women."

    44. "Sandra Day O'Connor, 1930 – ," www.greatwomen.org/ocnnor.htm, accessed July 21, 2000. "O'Connor, Sandra Day," Microsoft ® Encarta ® Online Encyclopedia 2000, http/encarta.msn.com. "Sandra Day O'Connor, Supreme Court Justice," www.who2.com/sandradayoconnor.html, accessed July 21, 2000. Garza, 1996, op.cit., front flap. Webster, op.cit., pp. 462-463. "Chapter One: The Right Woman," *Sandra Day O'Connor*, Peter Huber, www.phuber.com/huber/Sandra/sandch1.html, accessed August 14, 2000, p. 1.

    45. "Ginsburg, Ruth Bader," http://Encarta.msn.com/index/conciseindex/25/02566000.htm, accessed July 21, 2000. Garza, 1996, op.cit., pp. 9-10. Webster, op.cit., pp. 234-235.

    46. 'Geraldine Ferraro, 1935 - ," www.greatwomen.org/frraro.htm.

Chapter Six: Battling Still

    1. Krotz, Joanna L., "Getting Even: Why can't a woman be paid like a man? We examine the great salary divide – and what you can do to bridge it," *Working Woman*, July/August 1999, pp. 42-50. Wilson, Robin, "Timing is Everything: Academe's Annual Baby Boom," *The Chronicle of Higher Education*, June 25, 1999, pp. A14-A15. Jackson,

Maggie, "Minority women report obstacles," *Denver Rocky Mountain News*, July 14, 1999, p. 6B. "Small cracks key to glass ceiling," *The Denver Post*, January 7, 2000, p. 4C. McDonald, Kim A., "Studies of Women's Health Produce a Wealth of Knowledge on the Biology of Gender Differences," *The Chronicle of Higher Education*, June 25, 1999, pp. A 19 – A22.

2. Accola, John, "Most disputes never reach court," *Denver Rocky Mountain News*, March 30, 1999, p 8B.

3. "Facts About Sexual Harassment," The U.S. Equal Employment Opportunity Commission, www.eeoc.gov/facts/fs-Sex.html, accessed August 16, 2000. "Sexual Harassment: It's Not Academic," www.ed.gov/offices/OCR/ocrshpam.html, accessed August 16, 2000, p. 2.

4. Garland, Susan B., "Finally, A Corporate Tip Sheet on Sexual Harassment," *Business Week*, July 13, 1998, p. 39. The two 1998 landmark decisions from the Supreme Court are called *Faragher v. City of Boca Raton* and *Burlington Industries Inc. v. Ellerth*. Bryant, Margaret, "Ten Steps" Away From Sexual Harassment," Director's Monthly, August 1999, pp. 12-13.

5. Redwood, Rene, "The Glass Ceiling," www.inmotion.magazine.com/glass.html, accessed August 16, 2000, p. 2.

6. "Catalyst Study Finds Wage Gap Persists in Corporate Management," News Release, November 9, 1998, p. 1. "Executive Biographies: Carleton (Carly) S. Fiorina, President and Chief Executive Officer, Hewlett-Packard Company," www.hp.com/aboutp/newsroom/bios/fiorina.html, accessed August 16, 2000, p. 1. As of mid-2000, the number of women CEOs at Fortune 500 companies is back down to two—Jill Barad who was CEO of Mattel no longer is in that position. "Catalyst Reports Continued Gains for Women on Boards," *Director's Monthly*, July 1999, p. 15. 429 of the Fortune 500 companies now have at least one female director. More than one-third or 1,888 firms have more than one woman on their board. Only one Fortune 500 board has a majority of women directors—Golden West Financial Corporation, whose CEO is Marion Sandler. Diebel, Mary, "Despite gains, women face many barriers," *Denver Rocky Mountain News*,

March 7, 1999, pp. 1G and 18G.

7. Maupin, Rebekah J. and Cheryl R. Lehman, "Talking Heads: Stereotypes, Status, Sex-roles and Satisfaction—An Analysis of Female and Male Auditors," *Accounting, Organizations and Society*, Volume 19, Number 4/5 May/July 1994, p. 428 quotes Rosabeth Moss Kanter from her 1977 book *Men and Women of the Corporation*.

8. White, Joseph B. and Carol Hymowitz, "Watershed Generation of Women Executives Is Rising to the Top," The *Wall Street Journal*, February 10, 1997, pp. A1 and A8.

9. Zabarenko, Deborah, "Women Lead Men in Most Areas of Management, Study Indicates," The *Rocky Mountain News*, September 19, 1996, p. 7B. The study was conducted by the Foundation for Future Leadership. 6,000 questionnaires from 915 corporate workers were reviewed.

10. White and Hymowitz, op.cit., pp. A1 and A8.

11. Krotz, op.cit., p. 44.

12. Ibid, p. 42. "A Pay Cut For Women," *The Boston Globe*, September 16, 1997, p. A16.

13. Krotz, op.cit., p. 44. The high-profile legal victories for women include the 1999 award of $3.1 million in back pay and salary adjustments to female employees of Texaco, and the 1997 settlements of twin $80 million-plus awards against Home Depot and Publix Supermarkets. Kodak agreed to pay women employees a retroactive raise totaling several million dollars.

1999 *Working Women* Salary Survey
Median Earnings

Field	Women	Men	Overall
Accounting	32,136	42,692	35,048
Advertising - Large Firm	42,100	52,900	46,600
Advertising - Small Firm	40,500	50,600	45,000
Architecture	39,416	46,436	45,344
Clergy	24,856	31,356	31,148
Computers - System Analyst	46,280	51,792	49,504

Education - Professor, Ph.D.level	76,556	84,351	NA
Engineering - B.A. degree, 5-9 years	48,862	52,000	NA
Finance - Financial Managers	36,556	52,884	44,304
Graphic Design - Designers	29,224	37,440	33,020
Health Care Management - COO	69,954	87,325	81,000
Law - Lawyers	49,452	70,200	62,868
Magazine - Managing Editor 10+ years	51,426	50,810	NA
Medicine - Internist (general)	122,601	145,315	139,905
Medicine - General Surgeon	177,070	230,189	225,173
Newspapers - Editors & Reporters	32,032	42,224	37,596
Nursing - Registered Nurses	38,168	40,248	NA
Office Workers - Secretaries	25,480	26,624	25,532
Pharmacy - Hospital	56,950	60,950	59,491
Public Relations - Vice President	70,000	106,500	95,000
Publishing - Marketing Director	52,682	45,111	NA
Travel & Hospitality - Manager	31,800	39,600	33,400

14. Edmonds, Patricia, "Now the Word is Balance," *USA Weekend*, October 23-25, 1998, pp. 4-5. The survey was conducted by Liz Nickles and Laurie Ashcraft. Detailed, cross-referenced questions were sent to a statistically representative sample of 5,000 women ages 20-50 each time the survey was conducted.

15. Jackson, Maggie, "Women Start Own Firms in Frustration," *The Denver Post*, February 25, 1998, p. 3C. "Women-Owned Businesses Outpace All U.S. Firms," Press Release dated April 11, 1995, National Foundation for Women Business Owners, http://nfwbo.org/LocLink/BIZC/RESEARCH/LinkTo/4-11-1995/4-11/1995.htm, accessed August 21, 2000, p. 1.

16. Ibid. Schwab, Robert, "Women Executives Warn of Female Brain Drain," *The Denver Post*, March 17, 1998, p. 1C. Jackson, February 25, 1998, op.cit., p. 3C.

17. Swiss, Deborah J. and Judith P. Walker, *Women and the Work/Family Dilemma*, New York: John Wiley & Sons, 1993, pp. 19 and 23-25 Subtle forms of discrimination, so-called "micro-inequities" are destructive but nonactionable aspects of the work environment that occur at the level of individual decision-making. They are instances in which people are treated inequitably but not in a way that can be taken

to court. Examples include: not being given a challenging assignment that would lead to a promotion, not being asked to visit a particular client who represents the most significant income for the organization, not being included in social activities in which work is discussed, being subjected to comments on a continuing basis that are phrased humorously but are demeaning and other such actions—also called by some "water torture."

18. More, Ellen S., *Restoring the Balance: Women Physicians and the Profession of Medicine*, 1850-1995, Cambridge, Massachusetts: Harvard University Press, 1999, pp. 231 and 233.

19. "Family Medical Leave Act," www.doli.state.mn.us/fmla.html, accessed August 21, 2000, p. 1. Wilson, op.cit. However, academic women still feel significant pressure to time childbirth to coincide with summer break. Academic women may find this inconvenient and demeaning, however, this is a flexibility that many other working women do not have.

20. "Catalyst Study Finds Dual-Career Couples Want Freedom and Control: Would Leave Their Companies If They Don't Get It," Catalyst Press Release, January 20, 1998, www.catalystwomen.org/press/release0120.hml, p. 1. Ross, Sherwood, "As Job Stress Rises Worker Loyalty Falls," The *Rocky Mountain News*, July 12, 1998, p. 16G. "Aon Consulting Human resources Consulting Group," www.hrservices.aon.com, accessed November 27, 2000.

21. Jackson, Maggie, "Work-Family Study Finds Many Firms Without Policies," Associated Press Release in The *Denver Post*, July 15, 1998, p. 3C.

22. "Seeing Public Service as an Investment," *Newsweek*, May 4, 1992, p. 60.

23. Campbell, Mary, "Women of Independent Means: Business Advice From Owners of the Female Persuasion,"http://abcnews.go.com/sections/business/YourBusiness/sbb_000112.html, accessed August 16, 2000, p. 4. "Women-Owned Businesses Outpace All U.S. Firms," op.cit., p. 1.

24. "Credibility and Independence: Women Business Owners Voice Greatest Challenges and Biggest Rewards of Entrepreneurship," Press Release dated September 30, 1994, National Foundation for Women Business Owners, http://nfwbo.org/LocLink/BIZC/RESEARCH/LinkTo/9-30-1994/9-30-1994.htm, accessed August 21, 2000, p. 2.

Bibliography

Webster's Dictionary of American Women, New York: SMITHMARK Publishers, 1996.

Abrams, Ruth J. Ed., *Send Us a Lady Physician: Women Doctors in America, 1835-1920*, New York: W.W. Northon & Company, 1985.

Accola, John, "Most disputes never reach court," *Denver Rocky Mountain News*, March 30, 1999, p 8B.

Baer, Judith A., *Women in American Law: The Struggle Toward Equality From the New Deal to the Present*, 2nd Edition, New York: Homes & Meier, 1996.

Baldwin, Louis, *Women of Strength: Bibliographies of 106 Who Have Excelled in Traditionally Male Fields, A.D. 61 to the Present*, Jefferson, North Carolina: McFarland & Company, 1996.

Barbett, Samuel F. and Roslyn A. Korb, U.S. Department of Education, National Center for Education Statistics, Enrollment in Higher Education: Fall 1995, July 1997, NCES 97-440.

Blake, Kellee, "First in the Path of the Fireman: The Fate of the 1890 Population Census,"www.nara.gov/publications/prologue/1890cen1.html, accessed August 23, 2000.

Brackett, Anna C., editor. *Woman and The Higher Education.* New York: Harper and Brothers, 1893.

Bryant, Margaret, "Ten Steps" Away From Sexual Harassment," *Director's Monthly,* August 1999, pp. 12-13.

Burnham, Robert, "#8: The Code Napoleon," Frequently Asked Question (FAQ), The Napoleon Series, http://www.historyserver.org/napoleon.series/faq/c_code.html, accessed July 10, 2000.

Campbell, Mary, "Women of Independent Means: Business Advice From Owners of the Female Persuasion," http://abnews.go.com/sections/business/YourBusiness/sbb_000112.html, accessed August 16, 2000.

Chamberlain, Mariam K., Ed., *Women in Academe: Progress and Prospects,* New York: Russell Sage Foundation, 1988.

Clements, Jonathan, "The Many Ways to Play the Averages," *The Wall Street Journal,* March 28, 2000, p. C1.

Clinton, William J. A Proclamation by the President of the United States for Women's History Month 2000, March 2000.

Cromwell, Otelia, *Lucretia Mott,* Cambridge, Massachusetts: Harvard University Press, 1958.

D'Cruz, R. Jason, "Fair Labor Standards Act of 1938," www.mmmlaw.com/Articles/FairLaborStandardsAct of 1983.htm, accessed August 23, 2000.

Dexter, Elizabeth Anthony. *Career Women of America: 1776-1840,* Francetown, New Hampshire: Marshall Jones Company, 1950.

Diebel, Mary, "Despite gains, women face many barriers," *Denver Rocky Mountain News,* March 7, 1999, pp. 1G and 18G.

DuBois, Ellen, "Freedom: The Women's Rights Movement in a Word," Living the Legacy, National Women's History Project, 1998.

Edmonds, Patricia, "Now the Word is Balance," *USA Weekend,* October 23-25, 1998, pp. 4-5.

Farrell, Christopher, "Women in the Workplace: Is Parity Finally in Sight," *Business Week,* August 9, 1999, p. 35.

References

Flexner, Eleanor, *Century of Struggle: The Women's Rights Movement in the United States*, 2nd Edition, Cambridge, Massachusetts: Harvard University Press, 1975.

Flexner, Eleanor and Ellen Fitzpatrick, *Century of Struggle: The Women's Rights Movement in the United States*, Enlarged Edition, Cambridge, Massachusetts: The Belknap Press of Harvard University Press, 1996.

Foner, Philip S. and Josephine F. Pacheco, *Three Who Dared: Prudence Crandall, Margaret Douglass, Myrtilla Miner – Champions of Antebellum Black Education*, Westport, Connecticut: Greenwood Press, 1984.

Gallagher, Sean, "Federal Act prohibits unequal pay for equal work," *The Rocky Mountain News*, July 20, 1997, pp. 1J – 2J.

Garland, Susan B., "Finally, A Corporate Tip Sheet on Sexual Harassment," *Business Week*, July 13, 1998, p. 39.

Garza, Hedda, *Barred From the Bar: A History of Women in the Legal Profession*, New York: Franklin Watts, 1996.

Garza, Hedda, *Women in Medicine*, New York: Franklin Watts, 1994.

Gilchrist, Beth Bradford, *The Life of Mary Lyon*, New York: Houghton Mifflin Company, 1910.

Glazer, Penina Migdal and Miriam Slater, *Unequal Colleagues: The Entrance of Women Into the Professions, 1890 – 1940*, New Brunswick, New Jersey: Rutgers, University Press, 1987.

Harris, Barbara, *Beyond Her Sphere: Women in the Professions in American History*, Westport, Connecticut: Greenwood Press, 1978.

Hine, Darlene Clark, editor, *Black Women in United States History: Quest For Equality, The Life and Writings of Mary Eliza Church Terrell 1863-1954*, New York: Carlson Publishing, Inc., 1990.

Irwin, Inez Hayes, *The Story of Alice Paul and The National Woman's Party*, Fairfax, Virginia: Denlinger's Publishers, Ltd., 1977.

Jackson, Maggie, "Minority women report obstacles," *Denver Rocky Mountain News*, July 14, 1999, p. 6B.

Jackson, Maggie, "Women Start Own Firms in Frustration," *The Denver*

Post, February 25, 1998, p. 3C.

Jackson, Maggie, "Work-Family Study Finds Many Firms Without Policies," *The Denver Post*, July 15, 1998, p. 3C.

Jenkins, Joyce, "Amendments proposed to Fair Labor Standards Act," *Rocky Mountain News*, August 24, 1997, pp. 1J – 2J.

Kass-Simon, G., and Patricia Farnes, Editors, *Women of Science: Righting the Record*, Bloomington, Indiana: Indiana University Press, 1990.

Koerner, Brendan I., "Where the Boys Aren't," *U.S. News & World Report*, February 8, 1999, pp. 46-55.

Koretz, Gene, "Growing Gender Gap on Campus: Women's lead in enrollment is up," *Business Week*, February 15, 1999, p. 26.

Krotz, Joanna L., "Getting Even: Why can't a woman be paid like a man? We examine the great salary divide – and what you can do to bridge it," *Working Woman*, July/August 1999, pp. 42-50.

Lopez, Enrique Hank, *The Harvard Mystique: The Power Syndrome That Affects our Lives From Sesame Street to the White House*, New York: MacMillan Publishing Co., Inc., 1979.

Maupin, Rebekah J. and Cheryl R. Lehman, "Talking Heads: Stereotypes, Status, Sex-roles and Satisfaction – An Analysis of Female and Male Auditors," Accounting, Organizations and Society, 1993.

Maxwell, Joe, 'The Legacy of Booker T. Washington: A Family Reunion," November, 1996, http://www.capitalresearch.org/pcs/pcs-1196.html, accessed April 19, 2000.

Morello, Karen Berger, The Invisible Bar: The Woman Lawyer in America: 1638 to the Present, New York: Random House, 1986.

Read, Phyllis J. and Bernard L. Witlieb, *The Book of Women's Firsts*, New York: Random House, 1992.

Redwood, Rene, "The Glass Ceiling," www.inmotion.magazine.com/glass.html, accessed August 16, 2000.

Ried, Glenna E., Brenda T. Acken, and Elise G. Jancura, "An Historical Perspective of Women in Accounting," *Journal of Accountancy*, May 1987.

Rosenfeld, Isadore, Dr., "Why We're Healthier Today," *Parade Magazine*, March 19, 2000, pp. 4-6.

Ross, Sherwood, "As Job Stress Rises Worker Loyalty Falls," *The Rocky Mountain News*, July 12, 1998, p. 16G.

Rossi, Alice S. and Ann Calderwood, *Academic Women on the Move*, New York: Russell Sage Foundation, 1973.

Rossiter, Margaret W., *Women Scientists in America: Before Affirmative Action 1940-1972*, Baltimore, Maryland: The Johns Hopkins University Press, 1995.

Rossiter, Margaret W., *Women Scientists in America: Struggles and Strategies to 1940*, Baltimore, Maryland: The Johns Hopkins University Press, 1982.

Schroeder, Pat, *24 Years of House Work . . . and the Place is Still as Mess*, Kansas City: Andrews McMeel, 1998.

Schwab, Robert, "Women Executives Warn of Female Brain Drain," *The Denver Post*, March 17, 1998, p. 1C.

Seller, Maxine Schwartz, Ed., *Women Educators in the United States, 1820-1993*, Westport, Connecticut: Greenwood Press, 1994.

Silver, Sheryl, "Author Says Technical Skills Not Always a Must," *Los Angeles Times*, July 25, 1999, www.latimes.com/class/employ/silver/silv990725.htm, accessed August 31, 2000.

Stubblefield, Harold W. and Keane, Patrick, *Adult Education in the American Experience: From the Colonial Period to the Present*, San Francisco: Jossey-Bass, 1994.

Swiss, Deborah J. and Judith P. Walker, *Women and the Work/Family Dilemma*, New York: John Wiley & Sons, 1993.

Taylor, Dale, *The Writer's Guide to Everyday Life in Colonial America From 1607 – 1783*, Cincinnati, Ohio: Writer's Digest Books, 1997.

Tobias, Sheila, *Faces of Feminism: An Activist's Reflections on the Women's Movement*, Boulder, CO: Westview Press, 1997.

Uhland, Vicky, "Hospitality Managers Cash in," *Denver Rocky Mountain News*, April 4, 1999, pp. J1-2.

U.S. Department of Health and Human Services, "Women in Medicine," Council on Graduate Medicine Education, Fifth Report, July 1995.

U.S. Department of Labor, Women's Bureau, Fact Sheet on the Earnings Gap, Publication No. 71-86, 1971.

Wheeler, Marjorie Spruill, "The History of the Suffrage Movement," http://www.pbs.org/onewoman/suffrage.html, accessed April 28, 1999.

White, Joseph B. and Carol Hymowitz, "Watershed Generation of Women Executives Is Rising to the Top," *The Wall Street Journal*, February 10, 1997, p. A1 and A8.

Wilson, Robin, "Timing is Everything: Academe's Annual Baby Boom," *The Chronicle of Higher Education*, June 25, 1999, pp. A14-A15.

Zabarenko, Deborah, "Women Lead Men in Most Areas of Management, Study Indicates," *The Rocky Mountain News*, September 19, 1996, p. 7B.

Zinn, Howard, A People's History of the United States: 1492-Present, New York: Harper Perennial, 1995.

"III. The Gibbs Affair at Columbia College (1853-1854)," http:/beatl.barnard.columbia.edu/learn/GibbsAffair.htm, accessed August 29, 2000.

"1940s: GI Bill," www.stampsonline.com/century/40bill.htm, accessed July 20, 2000.

"About Carrie Chapman Catt," www.catt.org/ccabout.html, accessed July 10, 2000.

"Alice Paul 1885-1977," www.greatwomen.org/paul.htm, accessed July 11, 2000.

"Alpha Kappa Alpha: History – The Founders," www.aka1908.com/slowe.htm, accessed July 18, 2000.

"Amendments to the Constitution," http://www.law.emory/edu/FEDERAL/usconst/amend.html, accessed April 11, 2000.

References

"Anna Howard Shaw," www.multimag.com/state/mi/womens history/ahshaw/, accessed July 11, 2000.

"Anna Howard Shaw," www.multimag.com/state/mi/womenshistroy/ahshaw/bio.html, accessed July 31, 2000.

"Beecher, Catherine Esther (1800-1878), www.worldbook.com/fun/whm/html/whm090.html, accessed July 27, 2000.

"Betty Friedan," www.gale.com/freresrc/womenhst/friedan.htm, accessed July 20, 2000.

"Betty Friedan 1921 – ", www.greatwomen.org/frdan.htm, accessed July 20, 2000.

"Bridging Two Eras: The Autobiography of Emily Newell Blair, 1877-1951," Edited with an Introduction by Virginia Jeans Laas, http://system.missouri.edu/upress/fall1999/laas.htm, accessed July 18, 2000.

"*Brown v. Board of Education*," www.Watson.org/~lisa/blackhistory/early-civilrights/brown.html, accessed August 14, 2000.

"*Brown v. Board of Education of Topeka, Kansas*,"www.infoplease.com/ce5/CE007737.html, accessed July 14, 1999.

"Butler, Mother Marie Joseph," Encyclopaedia Brittanica, www.brittanica.com/seo/m/mother-marie-joseph-butler/, accessed July 18, 2000.

"Catalyst Reports Continued Gains for Women on Boards," *Director's Monthly*, July 1999, p. 15.

"Catalyst Study Finds Dual-Career Couples Want Freedom and Control: Would Leave Their Companies If They Don't Get It," Catalyst Press Release, January 20, 1998, www.catalystwomen.org/press/release0120.hml.

"Catalyst Study Finds Wage Gap Persists in Corporate Management," News Release, November 9, 1998.

"Catherine Beecher, 'Domestic Economy," www.depaul.edu/~clio/CBeecher.htm, accessed July 31, 2000.

"Chapter One: The Right Woman," Sandra Day O'Connor, Peter Huber, www.phuber.com/huber/Sandra/sandch1.html, accessed August 14, 2000.

"Code Napoléon," Microsoft ® Encarta ® Online Encyclopedia 2000, http://Encarta.msn.com © 1997-2000 Microsoft Corporation, accessed July 10, 2000.

"Coughlin v. Tailhook Association," www.lalabor.com/cases/shsa/tailhook1.html, accessed August 1, 2000.

"Credibility and Independence: Women Business Owners Voice Greatest Challenges and Biggest Rewards of Entrepreneurship," Press Release dated September 30, 1994, National Foundation for Women Business Owners, http://nfwbo.org/LocLink/BIZC/RESEARCH/LinkTo/9-30-1994/9-30-1994.htm, accessed August 21, 2000.

"A Curriculum of United States labor History for Teachers, sponsored by the Illinois Labor History Society, www.kentlaw.edu/his/curricul.htm, accessed July 20, 2000.

"Declaration of Sentiments," http://www.rochester.edu/SBA/declare.html, accessed March 9, 1999.

"Declaration of Sentiments, Seneca Falls, New York, 1848," http://www.closeup.org/sentiment.htm, accessed April 11, 2000.

"Democratic Party," http://Encarta.msn.com/find/Concise.asp?ti=02777000, accessed July 11, 2000

"Director's Gallery," www.dol.gov/dol/wb/gallery.htm, accessed July 20, 2000, p. 6.

"Edith Starrett Green," www.clerkweb.house/gov/womenbio/ExtendedBio/Green_edexb.htm, accessed July 20, 2000.

"Education Pays!" http://titan.iwu.edu/~jplath/booster.html.

"EEO/AA/Nondiscrimination Law & Policy for SDSU & SCW Institutions," www.sci.sdsu.edu/ODE/EEO_AA.html, accessed August 14, 2000.

"Elizabeth Cady Stanton 1815-1902," www.greatwomen.org/stanton.html, accessed July 11, 2000.

"Emma Willard School," http://www.emma.troy.ny.us, accessed March 14, 2000.

"Emma Willard School," www.cr.nps.gov/nr/travel/pwwmh/ny17.htm, accessed March 14, 2000

References

"Equal Pay Act of 1963," www.dot.gov/ost/docr/EQUALPAY.HTM, accessed July 21, 2000.

"Esther Peterson 1906-1997," www.greatwomen.org/ptrson.htm, accessed July 21, 2000.

"Excuse me, are women equal yet?" *Glamour*, February 1996, p. 91.

"Executive Biographies: Carleton (Carly) S. Fiorina, President and Chief Executive Officer, Hewlett-Packard Company," www.hp.com/aboutp/newsroom/bios/fiorina.html, accessed August 16, 2000.

"Facts About Sexual Harassment," The U.S. Equal Employment Opportunity Commission, www.eeoc.gov/facts/fs-Sex.html, accessed August 16, 2000.

"Family Medical Leave Act," www.doli.state.mn.us/fmla.html, accessed August 21, 2000.

"Geraldine Ferraro 1935 - ," www.greatwomen.org/frraro.htm, accessed August 1, 2000.

"Ginsburg, Ruth Bader," http://Encarta.msn.com/index/ conciseindex/25/02566000.htm, accessed July 21, 2000.

"Gloria Steinem," www.goddesscafe.com/FEMJOUR/steinem.html, accessed July 20, 2000.

"Gloria Steinem 1934 - ," www.greatwomen.org/stnem.htm, accessed July 20, 2000.

Heritage and Mission: Women's National Democratic Club, www.democraticwoman.org/heritage/, accessed July 18, 2000.

"History and Mission," www.gcc.edu/history/main.asp, accessed August 1, 2000.

history: biographies, William Randolph Hearst, www.hearstcastle.org/hearstcastle/bio_wrhearst.html, accessed July 7, 2000.

"History of Bilingual Education," Rethinking Schools, Volume 12, Number 3, Spring 1998, www.rethinkingschools.org/Archives/ 12_03/langhst.htm, accessed August 15, 2000.

History: The Founding of the University, www.Stanford.edu/home/ Stanford/history/begin.html, accessed July 7, 2000.

"Ida Bell Wells-Barnett 1862-1931," www.goddesscafe.com/FEMJOUR/wells.html, accessed July 11, 2000.

"Ida Wells-Barnett 1862-1931," www.greatwomen.org/wbrnett.htm, accessed July 11, 2000.

"Information for High School Students," www.saintmarys.edu/!incandel/highschool.html, accessed July 18, 2000.

" 'Jim Crow' Laws", http://www.nps.gov/malu/documents/jim_crow_laws.htm, accessed April 20, 2000.

"Josephine St. Pierre Ruffin 1842-1924," www.greatwomen.org/ruffin.htm, accessed July 11, 2000.

"Julia Clifford Lathrop," Microsoft ® Encarta ® 96 Encyclopedia. © 1993-1995 Microsoft Corporation, © Funk & Wagnalls Corporation, www.netsrq.com/~dboise/lathrop.html, accessed July 18, 2000.

"The Land Grant System of Education in the United States," http://www.ag.ohio-state.edu/~ohioline/lines/lgrant.html, accessed April 11, 2000.

"Legacy of Women Subject of Tuskegee University Research With Support of State Humanities Grant," http://www.tusk.edu/news_info/new/women.htm, accessed, April 19, 2000.

"Lucretia Mott 1793-1880," www.greatwomen.org/mott.htm, accessed July 11, 2000.

"Lucy Stone 1818-1893," www.greatwomen.org/stone.htm, accessed July 11, 2000.

"Mary Lyon 1797-1849," www.greatwomen.org.lyon.htm, accessed July 27, 2000.

"Mary McLeod Bethune 1875-1955," www.greatwomen.org, accessed July 18, 2000.

"Mary McLeod Bethune Legacy Continuation Foundation, Inc.," http://users.erols.com/trirose/Bethune/Bethune.htm, accessed July 18, 2000.

"Miriam Leslie: Belle of the Boardroom," From *Smithsonian Magazine*, November 1997, http://www.smithsonianmag.si.edu/s...n/issues97/nov97/Miriam_nov97.html.

References

"The Nineteenth Amendment and the War of the Roses in Nashville," wysiwyg://16http://www.blueshoenashville.com/suffragehistory.html, accessed July 11, 2000.

"Notice: Impacts of the Civil Rights Restoration Act of 1987 on FHWA Programs, www.fhwa.dot.gov/legsregs/directives/notices/n4720-6.htm, accessed August 1, 2000.

"NPG Facts and Figures: Historical U.S. Population Growth by year 1900-1998," www.npg.org/facts/us_historical_pops.htm, accessed August 23, 2000.

"O'Connor, Sandra Day," Microsoft ® Encarta ® Online Encyclopedia 2000, http/encarta.msn.com.

"The Organic Act of the Department of Labor," www.dol.gov/dol/asp/public/programs/history/organact.htm, accessed July 20, 2000.

"A Pay Cut For Women," The Boston Globe, September 16, 1997, p. A16.

"People & Events: Nannie Helen Burroughs," www.pbs.org/wg...1900/peopleevents/pandeAMEX43.html, accessed July 18, 2000.

"Peterson, Esther," Encyclopaedia Brittanica, www.brittanica.com/seo/e/esther-peterson/, accessed July 21, 2000.

"Picture of the Day," February 28, The GI Bill, www.britishheritage.com/picture/0228.htm, accessed August 30, 2000.

"President, First Lady Saddened At Death of Esther Peterson," News Release, December 23, 1997.

"Profiles in Caring: Mary McLeod Bethune 1875-1955," www.nahc.org/NAHC/Val/Columns/SC10-6.html, accessed August 1, 2000

"Prudence Crandall 1803-1890," www.ctforum.org/cwhf/crandall.htm, accessed July 27, 2000.

"Rankin, Jeannette, 1880-1973," http://bioguide.cogress.gov/scripts/biodisplay.pl?index=R000055, accessed August 1, 2000.

"Republican Party, http://Encarta.msn.com/find/Concise.asp?ti-04241000, accessed July 11,2000.

Sandra Day O'Connor, 1930 – ," www.greatwomen.org/ocnnor.htm, accessed July 21, 2000.

"Sandra Day O'Connor, Supreme Court Justice," www.who2.com/sandradayoconnor.html, accessed July 21, 2000.

"Seeing Public Service as an Investment," Newsweek, May 4, 1992, p. 60.

Senate Reports, 78th Congress, 1st Session, January 6 – December 21, 1943, Volume 2, Calendar No. 372, Report 363.

"Senate Statistics: Women in the Senate," www.senate.gov/learning/stat_14.html, accessed August 1, 2000

"Sexual Harassment: It's Not Academic," www.ed.gov/offices/OCR/ocrshpam.html, accessed August 16, 2000.

"Small cracks key to glass ceiling," The Denver Post, January 7, 2000, p. 4C.

"Sojourner Truth c.1797-1883," www.greatwomen.org/truth.htm, accessed July 11, 2000.

"Steinem, Gloria," an Encarta Encyclopedia article, http://Encarta.msn.com/index/conciseindex/1F/01F59000.htm?z=1@pg=2&br=1, accessed July 20, 2000.

"Summary of Federal Laws," http://counsel.cua.edu/fedlaw/CR1987.htm, accessed August 1, 2000.

"Susan Brownell Anthony 1820-1906," www.greatwomen.org/anthony.htm, accessed July 11, 2000.

"Tailhook Incident," www.now.org/issues/military/policies/tailhk.html, accessed August 1, 2000.

Title IX of the Education Amendments of 1972 prohibits Discrimination Based on Sex in Education Programs or Activities which Receive Federal Financial Assistance," www.ed.gov/offices/OCR/tix_dis.html, accessed August 23, 2000.

"Tuskegee Institute: National Historic Site," http://www.nps.gov/tuin/, accessed April 19, 2000.

"U.S. Supreme Court – Law v. Nichols, 414 U.S. 563 (1974)," http://caselaw.findlaw...rt=US&navby=case&vol=414&invol=563, accessed August 15, 2000.

"War Jobs for Women", Office of War Information, Magazine Section, Washington, DC, undated.

"What court rulings have impacted the education of language minority students in the U.S.?," www.ncbe.gwu.edu/askncbe/faqs/07court.htm, accessed August 15, 2000.

"Who We Are," www.natlconsumersleague.org/whoweare.htm, accessed July 21, 2000.

"Winning the Right to Vote," www.greatwomen.org/lcvt.htm, accessed July 11, 2000.

"WLB: What It Is . . . How It Operates," A-2381, published by the National War Labor Board, undated.

"Women Builders – Nannie Helen Burroughs," nttp://nmaatyder.si.edu/Johnson/burrough.html, accessed July 18, 2000.

"Women-Owned Businesses Outpace All U.S. Firms," Press Release dated April 11, 1995, National Foundation for Women Business Owners, http://nfwbo.org/LocLink/BIZC/RESEARCH/LinkTo/4-11-1995/4-11/1995.htm, accessed August 21, 2000.

"Women in Congress: Congresswomen's Biographies," http://bioguide.congress.gov/congresswomen/index.asp, accessed August 1, 2000.

http://bioguide.congress.gov/biosearch/biosearch1.asp, accessed July 21, 2000.

Index

Abolition, 20-21, 23-25, 36-37, 39, 48, 52, 57, 69, 74, 89-91, 94, 97, 109, 120
Academia, women in, 53, 114
Accounting, women in, 53
Adams, Abigail, 13
Adams, John, 13
Addams, Jane, 106
Advancement, 158-162, 164-165, 172, 203 n.6
Affirmative action, 124, 134-135, 137, 147, 150-152, 195 n. 44, 202 n. 43
African-American education, 19-21, 35-36, 48, 52-53, 56-57, 98-99, 113, 115, 128, 144, 191 n. 19, 200-201 n. 26
Age of Reform, 39
American and Foreign Anti-Slavery Society, 25
American Association of University Women, 105, 151
American Civil Liberties Union, 67, 154
American Equal Rights Association, 78, 89, 96-97
American Woman Suffrage Association, 78-79, 89, 93, 96, 98
Anthony amendment, 78, 86, 92-94, 106
Anthony, Susan B., 24, 43-44, 74, 78-79, 96-98, 100-102, 185,-186 n. 42
Antioch College, 46
Anti-Slavery Society, 94
Association of Collegiate Alumnae, 60
Barber-Scotia College, 53, 128
Barnett, see Wells-Barnett, Ida
Barnhart, Henry, 87
Beecher, Catherine, 22, 33-34, 37
Bennett College, 53
Bethune, Albertus L., 128

Bethune, Mary McLeod, 113, 128-129
Bethune-Cookman College, 128
Bilingual Education Act of 1968, 143
Bittenbinder, Ada, 64-65
Blackwell, Alice Stone, 79, 94
Blackwell, Elizabeth, 61-62, 94
Blackwell, Henry, 79, 94-95
Blair, Emily Newell, 110, 114-115, 190 n. 2
Bloomer, Amelia, 97
Bradwell, Myra, 54-55
Breckenridge, Sophonisa, 67
Brown, Antoinette, (later known as Antoinette Brown Blackwell) 18, 94
Brown v. Board of Education, 105, 142-143
Brown, Linda, 142
Bryn Mawr College, 3, 23, 46, 50
Burke, Edmund, 15
Burn, Harry, 87
Burns, Lucy, 106
Burroughs, Nannie, 113
Business administration, women in, 137, 144, 148-149, 166
Butler, Mother Marie Joseph, 113
Caraway, Hattie Wyatt, 141
Catt, Carrie Chapman, 71, 83-85, 98, 100-102
Catt, George, 101
Childcare, 115-116, 118, 124-125, 127, 130, 165, 169-170
Child custody, 27, 54, 70, 83, 92, 95, 97
Civil death, 10, 14, 27, 29
Civil Rights Act, 123-124, 133, 136, 139, 141, 143, 159

Civil rights movement, 24, 109, 120, 124, 143-144
Civil Rights Restoration Act, 140-141
Code Nalpolean, 82, 184-185 n. 37
Colby, Bainbridge, 87
Collins, Eileen, 202 n.43
Colored Women's League of Washington, 99
Columbia University, 153-154
Combe, George, 18-19
Community, colleges, 142, 145
Congressional Union for Woman Suffrage, 106
Coughlin, Paula A., 140
Crandall, Prudence, 34-36, 56-57
Cult of domesticity, 23
Cult of true womanhood, 4, 37
Dame schools, 16-17, 176 n. 31
Dartmouth College, 12
Declaration of Independence, 13, 26
Declaration of Sentiments, 25-29, 40-41, 89, 92
Divorce laws, 27, 40, 54, 70, 82-83, 92, 97, 111
Doctorates, 49-50, 59-60, 114-116, 118, 144, 191-192 n. 19
Douglass, Frederick, 29, 44, 57, 90, 97, 103
DuBois, W.E.B., 52
Dyer, Mary, 11
Eastman, Crystal, 67
Eclectic Central Medical College, 62
Education Amendments of 1972, 136, 142
Emma Willard School, 30
Engineering, women in, 53, 114, 144-145, 148

English Common Law, 10
Equal Credit Opportunity Act, 138
Equal Educational Opportunity Act of 1974, 143
Equal Employment Opportunity Act of 1972, 136
Equal Employment Opportunity Commission, 124, 136, 139, 151
Equal Pay Act, 121-123, 129, 133, 136, 139, 143, 162
Equal rights, 39-40, 54, 62, 66, 82, 94, 107, 110, 121-122, 124-125, 127, 130, 152
Equal Rights Amendment, 107, 118, 124-127, 130, 177 n. 55
Executive Order 11246, 134
Executive Order 11375, 134-135
Faculty, women, 112, 114-116, 135, 145, 154, 157, 206 n. 19
Fair Labor Standards Act, 122
Fairchild, James, 17
Family and Medical Leave Act, 167
Federal Glass Ceiling Commission, 160
Federal Reserve Board, 138
Felton, Rebecca Latimer, 141
Female Anti-Slavery Society, 88
Female Medical College of Pennsylvania, 61
Female seminaries, 16
Feminism, 111, 117-120, 123-125, 127, 136, 141-142, 146, 151-152, 179 n. 4
Ferraro, Geraldine, 141, 154-155
Foster, J. Ellen, 64
Franklin, Benjamin, 4
Franklin, Deborah, 4

Free Religious Association, 89
Friedan, Betty, 119-120, 124, 130-131
G.I. Bill, 116, 192-193 n. 22
Gage, Frances Dana, 90-91
Gage, Mathilda Joslyn, 185-186 n. 42
General Federation of Women's Clubs, 103
Geneva Medical College, 62
Giles, Harriet, 52
Ginsburg, Ruth Bader, 133, 142, 153-154
Graduate education programs, 49-50, 59-60, 112, 144
Green, Edith, 121, 136, 194 n. 41
Griffiths, Martha, 195 n. 41
Grimke, Sarah, 24, 36-37
Grove City College, 140-141, 199 n. 19
Harper, Ida Husted, 81, 185-186 n. 42
Harvard University, 12, 32, 46, 51, 61, 99, 153, 167
Haskell, Ella, 66
Hearst, Millicent, 81
Hearst, William Randolph, 81
Hicks, Frederick, 87
Hill, Anita, 133, 139-140, 198 n. 16
Home economics, 58-59
Houston Tillotson College, 53
Howard University, 35, 105
Howe, Julia Ward, 79, 99
Hunt, Harriot, 61-62
Hunt, Sarah, 61
Hutchinson, Anne, 10-11
Industrial Revolution, 21, 23
Ingalls, John, 66

Interdepartmental Committee of the Status of Women, 121
International Women Suffrage Association, 102
Jacobi, see Putnam-Jacobi, Mary
Jefferson, Thomas, 13, 187 n. 54
Jim Crow laws, 72, 182-183 n. 9
Johns Hopkins University, 50, 60
Johnson, Lyndon Baines, 134-135
Kennedy, John F., 120-121, 162
Kepley, Ada, 64
Labor reforms, 22, 67, 76-77, 121, 125-127, 186 n. 47, 193 n. 26
Ladd-Franklin, Christine, 59-60
Lau v. Nichols, 143
Law, women in, 28, 53-56, 63-67, 84, 114, 117, 137, 144, 149-150, 163, 166
Laws of Coverture, 55
League of Nations, 100-102, 107
League of Women Voters, 102, 110
Lease, Mary, 65-66
Leslie, Miriam, 83-84
Life/work balance, 158, 163-170
Lincoln, Abraham, 91, 187 n. 54
Lozier, Clemence Sophia, 62
Lyon, Mary, 31-32
Mann, James, 87
Martin, Ellen, 65
Marymount School, 113
McCarthy era, 120
McCulloch, Catherine, 67
Medicine, women in, 28, 53-54, 60-63, 84-85, 114, 116-117, 136-137, 144, 149, 163, 166-167, 191 n. 15
Mexican-American eduction, 53, 200-201 n. 26
Miner, Myrtilla, 56-57
Minick, Alice, 65
Moody Bible Institute, 128
Morella, Connie, 202 n. 43
Morrill Act of 1862, 180 n. 22
Mott, James, 89
Mott, Lucretia, 24-26, 88-89, 91-92, 125, 195 n. 47
Mount Holyoke College, 31-32, 36, 45-46, 50, 64, 178 n. 64, 179 n. 18
Murray, Judith Sargent, 15
Mutual Improvement Societies, 21
National Afro-American Council, 104
National American Woman Suffrage Association, 79, 83, 85-87, 93, 96, 98, 100-102, 106
National Association for the Advancement of Colored People, 104
National Association of Colored Women, 99, 105
National League of Republican Colored Women, 113
National Organization for Women, 119, 124-126, 130, 138
National War Labor Board, 116
National Woman Suffrage Association, 78-79, 89, 92-93, 98, 100
National Woman's Party, 106-107, 110, 125, 195 n. 47
National Women's Political Caucus, 130-131
Native American education, 19-20, 48, 53, 200-201 n. 26
Negro Fellowship League, 104

New England Hospital for Women and Children, 62
New England Women's Club, 99
New York Academy of Medicine, 63
New York Infirmary for Women and Children, 62
New York Medical College and Hospital for Women, 63
Oberlin College, 17-18, 46, 94, 104-105
O'Connor, Sandra Day, 133, 141, 152-153
Office of Federal Contract Compliance, 135
Packard, Sophie, 52
Paine, Thomas, 14
Paul, Alice, 83-84, 105-107, 125, 195 n. 47
Perry, Mary Frederick, 65
Peterson, Esther, 120-121, 129
Pierce, Sarah, 17
Plessy v. Ferguson, 142, 199-200 n. 23
Presidential Commission of the Status of Women, 120-121, 129
Preston, Ann, 61
Princeton University, 12, 46
Public education, 11-12, 45
Putnam-Jacobi, Mary, 63
Quakers and African-American education, 20-21, 48, 56-57
Radcliffe College, 51
Rankin, Jeannette, 141
Reagan, Ronald, 141-142, 153, 155
Richard, Ellen Henrietta Swallow, 58-59
Rosie the Riveter, 115

Roosevelt, Eleanor, 118, 121, 126
Roosevelt, Franklin D., 116
Roosevelt, Franklin D., Jr., 124
Rousseau, Jean-Jacques, 11
Ruffin, George L., 99
Ruffin, Josephine St. Pierre, 98-99
Ruch, Benjamin, 15
St. Mary's College, 113
Sandler, Bernice, 135
Sargent, Senator A.A., 78
Schlafly, Phyllis, 126
Schroeder, Pat, 138
Sciences, women in, 53, 148
Seneca Falls Convention (New York), 25-26, 29, 40, 44, 71, 88-89, 92, 96
Sex discrimination, 54, 123-124, 135, 137-140, 151, 162, 163
Sexual harassment, 139-140, 151, 158-159, 198 n. 15
Shaw, Anna Howard, 87, 100-102, 106, 114-115
Sheppard-Towner Act, 111
Shuler, Nettie Rogers, 71
Sims, Thetus, 86-87
Slave codes, 20
Slowe, Lucy Diggs, 113
Smith College, 32, 46, 50, 130-131, 179 n. 20
Smith, Howard, 123
Southern chivalry, 73
Spelman College, 52, 200-201 n. 26
Stanford, Jane, 81
Stanford, Leland, 81
Stanford University, 81, 152
Stanton, Elizabeth Cady, 24-26, 43-44, 74, 78-79, 88, 91-93, 96-97, 109, 185-186, n. 42

Stanton, Henry, 25, 91
State and Local Fiscal Assistance Act of 1972, 139
Steinem, Gloria, 119-120, 131
Stone, Lucy, 18, 43-44, 78-79, 93-96, 99
Stowe, Harriet Beecher, 22, 33, 57
Strickland, Martha, 66
Tailhook, 140
Tammany Hall, 76, 183-184 n. 22
Teaching, as profession for women, 31, 33, 47, 49, 57, 97, 103, 114, 150
Temperance movement, 55, 63-65, 67, 69, 97, 100, 183 n. 20
Terrell, Mary Church, 74, 104-105
Texas A&M University, 112
Theology, women in, 28, 144
Thomas, Clarence, 7, 133, 139, 198 n. 16
Thomas, M. Carey, 50
Troy Female Seminary, 30-31, 46, 91
Truth, Sojourner, 89-91
Tuskegee Insititute, 52-53, 105
Underground Railroad, 65, 89
United Nations, 107
U.S. Constitution, 13-14, 41-44, 70-72, 74, 77-78, 86-88, 97-98, 101-102, 106, 109, 111, 122, 126-127, 136, 143, 188 n. 55, 196 n. 50
University of Virginia, 112
Vassar College, 32, 46, 67
Washington, Booker T., 52, 105
Washington, George, 12, 187 n. 54
Washington, Margaret Murray, 105
Webster, Noah, 15
Weekend colleges, 147
Weld, Angelina Grimke, 24, 36-37

Wellesley College, 32, 46, 50
Wells-Barnett, Ida, 102-104
Wheatley, Phillis, 12-13
White, Walter, 74
Wilberforce College, 105
Willard, Emma Hart, 29-31
Willard, Frances, 63-64
Willard, John, 30
Wilson, Woodrow, 84, 86, 100, 103, 106
Wolff, Sister Madeleva, 113
Wollstonecraft, Mary, 14-15, 22-23
Woman's Party, 106
Women in Congress, ii
Women in the professions, 40-41, 49-51, 53-56, 70, 84, 112, 114, 117-118, 133, 137-138, 144-145, 151, 158-159, 166, 172, 180 n. 28
Women-owned businesses, 151, 158, 161, 163-165, 170-172
Women's Bureau, 120, 129, 193-194 n. 35
Women's clubs, 75, 103, 105, 115
Women's clubs, African-American, 99, 103, 105
Women's colleges, 32, 46, 49-50, 52-53, 112-113
Women's education, 15-16, 28, 37, 39, 45-48, 69-70, 77, 84, 112-113, 115-116, 121, 125, 136-138, 142-149
Women's Equity Action League, 135-136
Women's Era Club, 99
Women's Joint Congressional Committee, 111
Women's rights, 22-24, 26, 29, 36-